SQL Wait Stats
Joes 2 Pros®

SQL Performance Tuning Techniques
Using Wait Statistics, Types & Queues

By

Pinal Dave
Founder of SQLAuthority.com

Rick A. Morelan
Founder of Joes2Pros.com

© Pinal Dave/Rick A. Morelan
All Rights Reserved 2011

ISBN: 1-4662-3477-6
EAN: 978-1-4662-3477-2

*To my lovely daughter, Shaivi Dave, and
my understanding wife, Nupur Dave*

– Pinal Dave

Table of Contents

About the Authors

Pinal Dave

Pinal works as a Technology Evangelist with Microsoft India. He has been a part of the IT industry for more than seven years. During his career he has worked both in India and the US, primarily with SQL Server Technology - right from version 6.5 to its latest form. Pinal has worked on many performance tuning and optimization projects for high transactional systems. He received his Master of Science from the University of Southern California and a Bachelors of Engineering from Gujarat University. Additionally, he holds many Microsoft certificates. He has been a regular speaker at many international events like TechEd, SQL PASS, MSDN, TechNet, and countless user groups.

Pinal writes frequently on his blog http://blog.SQLAuthority.com on various subjects concerning SQL Server technology and Business Intelligence. His passion for the community drives him to share his training and knowledge. Before joining Microsoft, he was awarded the Microsoft Most Valuable Professional (MVP) in SQL Server Technology for three continuous years for his outstanding community service. He was also awarded the Community Impact Award – Individual Contributor for Y2010. When he is not in front of a computer, he is usually travelling to explore hidden treasures in nature with his toddler daughter, Shaivi, and very supportive wife, Nupur.

Rick Morelan

In 1994 you could find Rick Morelan braving the frigid waters of the Bering Sea as an Alaska commercial fisherman. His computer skills were non-existent at the time, so you might not imagine such beginnings would lead him to SQL Server expertise at Microsoft. However, every computer expert in the world today woke up at some point in his or her life knowing nothing about computers. They say luck is what happens when preparation meets opportunity. In the case of Rick Morelan, people were a big part of his good luck.

Making the change from the fishing industry seemed scary and took daily schooling at Catapult Software Training Institute. Rick got his lucky break in August 1995, working his first database job at Microsoft. Since that time, Rick has worked more than 10 years at Microsoft and has attained over 30 Microsoft technical certifications in applications, networking, databases, and .NET development.

Acknowledgements

Authors are a bit like astronauts – when launch time ignites, they get all the glory and grace the cover of each printed book that records their heroic endeavor. Extraordinary talents are in people everywhere around us. For every need we've encountered, talented and motivated people have come out of the woodwork and showed up at just the right moment to support this effort. In this section, we want to pay tribute to core people who made the process happen:

Editors: Jessica Brown, Brandon Nelson
Content Review: Joel Heidal, Simon Nicholson
Website & Digital Marketing: Blue Digital Media

Introduction

Pick something in your life that you have mastered and can do with ease. Many people pick the topic of driving. You know how to turn left while slowing down. You are tuning many controls at once and getting feedback from your vehicle to make it run and move toward your intended destination. An occasional glance at the fuel gauge tells you when to visit the fueling station. If you tried to be highly skilled at driving without knowing what all these gauges and levers did, it would be nearly impossible and you would have to rely heavily on the advice of others to make simple decisions.

So it's true with SQL that knowing how a few gauges and levers work can prompt you to take simple actions or confidently know you have everything set for right now. Yet most SQL systems that we've encountered have simple problems. Imagine your car's tire pressure gauge is way below tolerance levels and instead of a simple adjustment, the system keeps running until it breaks.

New knowledge also replaces the dangers of taking the wrong action or diagnosing the wrong cause of a problem. For example, when you see the fuel gauge in your car, you take action. That gauge is a tool for your benefit and not some evil thing that only bears bad news. A fuel gauge saying you are full is good news. Throwing away or painting over the gauge won't make the bad juju go away.

You learn a lot when thrown into a crisis situation, where everyone is looking to you for answers. The system is down, the CEO is pleading to you for answers, as each minute of downtime further cuts into the company's bottom line. You can almost hear the fiscal charts turning upside down. The simple fix you thought would work when you received the call will not fix the scenario you've just walked into. In a hurry, you need new ideas right away.

The seconds you spend scratching your head surrounded by six panicking people can seem like hours. Once you find the answers, you will remember them for a long time and be better equipped to help your next client group. The good news is you can learn some

8

of these answers by reading. When you encounter the same situations, you will know exactly what to do.

Let this book be your helpful tool in your work. When used correctly, it can help you can determine solutions relating to these relatively simple (yet lesser known) areas of SQL Server. It has been polished and tuned for your use and benefit. In fact, this is the book I really wished was in my possession prior to some of those not-so-fun days I've just described.

Skills Needed for this Book

This book assumes at least an intermediate knowledge of SQL Server. This can be from a combination of experience and training. You need to already have a knowledge of queries, programming objects (like tables and stored procedures), and indexes. If you are new to the field but have done extensive studies, then this book assumes you have been exposed to the concepts in the first four of the five SQL *Joes 2 Pros* SQL development books:

Beginning SQL Joes 2 Pros: The SQL Hands-On Guide for Beginners
ISBN 1-4392-5317-X

SQL Queries Joes 2 Pros: SQL Query Techniques for Microsoft SQL Server 2008
ISBN 1-4392-5318-8

SQL Architecture Basics Joes 2 Pros: Core Architecture Concepts
ISBN: 1-4515-7946-2

SQL Programming Development Joes 2 Pros: Programming & Development for Microsoft SQL Server 2008
ISBN: 1-4515-7948-9

SQL Interoperability Joes 2 Pros: SQL 2008 Techniques with XML, C#, and PowerShell
ISBN: 1-4515-7950-0

About this Book

When you see the word "I" followed by a business or client example, it will be a first person experience account from author Pinal Dave during his vast experience consulting in the field. Some of the experiences of Rick Morelan will be added as concepts.

Bear in mind that the study of wait types is a vast subject, and it would be difficult for one person to understand every wait type and its associated statistics. SQL Server 2008 R2 includes nearly 500 wait types, and this number will increase in the next version of SQL Server (codename "Denali").

Wait types are not new to SQL Server but the techniques to interpret this feature are not widely available. Performance tuning has been a mainstream concern for SQL professionals for many years. There are many tactics which experts use to tune servers, queries, and systems; however, techniques for using wait types, wait queues, and wait statistics in performance tuning are understood by relatively few in our industry.

This book is a humble attempt to make these concepts more accessible to SQL developers. We consider this book a first version of the ongoing research in this area. Of the hundreds of wait types, this book covers the most visible ones. This initial volume doesn't cover the wait statistics with less significance or ones seldom seen. Again, every wait type potentially has multiple solutions and we have attempted to cover the common solutions.

While you read and implement suggestions, we highly recommend that you attempt them first on your development server before implementing them on your production server.

Please send us feedback as you try out various solutions based on the wait types. We will incorporate your experience in a future version of the book, which will include an expanded write up with more real world scenarios and many more wait types.

Chapter 1. Introduction to Wait Stats

What do you consider to be some of the most useful inventions? Common answers generally include the light bulb, the elevator, or even the aqueduct (we all need water). These are generally good things whose benefits become even more meaningful to us, once we learn how they can be utilized.

Understanding these tools well, we find that light bulbs and elevators are frequently used by us. A movie about a pregnant woman getting stuck all night in an elevator wouldn't scare us away from using these beneficial features. Our familiarity with elevators means we know the upsides and downsides of using elevators.

Seeing the terms "wait" or "waiting" in the context of a server system may give the impression that wait stats are indicators of something bad happening to your system. In fact they are simply another invention (or feature), and oftentimes they actually tell you that everything is good and running smoothly.

Consider some everyday situations where waiting can actually help increase the efficiency of a process. If a bus is going to let 30 people off at the main station, that can happen quickly if the bus stops and waits with the door held open. All the passengers can get off very quickly. If the bus merely slowed down, people would need to very carefully jump off one at a time. The bus would actually help fewer people (and maybe even injure a few!) by not waiting. Adding this short wait makes the bus more productive. Including waits with other SQL Server options can actually improve and speed up overall performance.

This book will focus on how to view wait stats and make the waits work for us. Doctors tell us there is good cholesterol and bad cholesterol, and we believe them. Take our word for it: we will help you identify the good and bad wait stats and what actions to take in either situation.

SQLAuthority.com
Joes2Pros.com

Your Natural Skills

Each new version of SQL Server includes cool, new features and optimization of existing features. With each new release, I can't wait to learn what problems the new version solves and what new features are available. Knowing people will ask me about how new features work, I'm always eager to look "under the hood" and understand just how SQL Server is accomplishing each new capability. I've been doing this for several years, and each time I do this, my study tends to reinforce an observation I made a few years ago: the brilliant, new SQL Server feature is actually not complex. In most cases, I find that basic common sense has been used to add new logic and improve the software which comprises SQL Server.

This continuous improvement of SQL Server reminds me of something most readers will have observed when visiting a large grocery store. Any cashier has the essential ability to inventory your items, tally up your order total, and accept your payment for the items you have chosen. At the same time cashiers conduct these basic transactions, you can observe them simultaneously performing another subtle but critical business function beyond just being a productive cashier.

Businesses have learned that the less time they make you wait in line, the more likely you are to buy today and enjoy your shopping experience, which makes it more likely that you will view the experience favorably and return to shop there again. In most cities and neighborhoods, you have another nearby store you could easily choose instead. For this reason, you will notice the cashier (while talking to you and handling your purchase) is occasionally looking around to the queue of shoppers waiting to buy. If this line of shoppers becomes too long, the cashier will pick up the internal store microphone and page another cashier to come to the front of the store. The additional employee also performs cashier duties until customer wait times are reduced.

When you see a busy cashier stop processing transactions and pick up the store intercom, you know help is on the way. During the five seconds it takes to summon a new cashier, no customers are being served. Despite the fact that no transactions are progressing, the five second wait is welcomed because it signals that everyone's transactions will be completed faster.

Even if there is nobody else in line, you will still encounter a few productive waits. If your payment method requires a network transaction (e.g., if you pay with a debit/credit card), then you will experience at least a momentary wait for the network transaction to complete. If you pay with cash, then you will experience a wait while they count your change and give you a receipt. These are good waits for you, because each small wait we've described actually works to benefit you. However, you would not benefit from waiting if cashiers stopped processing transactions and instead worked on end of shift paperwork. Preventing one or more tills from processing while customers stand waiting for several minutes is not pleasant – if that happened, you could say that would be the wrong type of wait. A basic rule is that too many of the wrong kind of waits (also known as *wait types*) are bad for business.

Most of us have seen this commonplace grocery store observation. Common sense tells us that adding efficiency to the store makes for good business and happy consumers. When an overwhelmed store with one cashier calls on a new cashier to save us waiting time, we are appreciative. But are we amazed at this brilliance, since to us it seems like simple common sense and customer courtesy?

If a store manager says, "I want to monitor the number of people waiting. If there are more than 10, then we know there is too much pressure on the current cashier staff to handle customers in a timely fashion", you would agreed that is a good decision. Yet when I as a SQL developer say something like, "I want to monitor the runnable_tasks_count and if I get a two digit number or higher (i.e., 10 or greater), then CPU pressure is causing performance problems", people are amazed and pay me good money. My point is that you already have this brilliance – all that needs to be done now is to make it obvious and put your common sense to work.

Once you understand how SQL Server's processes work together – the same way you intuitively understand the cashier and customer process patterns in a grocery store – your common sense can make you appear to be a SQL wiz. What we must do next is to make SQL Server's processes more familiar to you.

The goal of this chapter is to take you a step further toward a level of expertise where a quick glance at the "grocery store" of SQL Server gives you a true sense of what is going on and which steps you can take next in good practice. Wait types are vital to measuring performance bottlenecks.

What are Wait Stats

At the start of a road trip with family or friends, we wait until everyone has gotten into the car and buckled their safety belts before we start driving. The time it takes for passengers to buckle up requires only a short wait, and it is wise to wait until everyone is ready for takeoff. To drive off and not wait would be irresponsible (and even illegal in some parts of the world). You gladly wait to for your "driving task" to start only after the "fasten all safety belts" task is done.

Whenever SQL Server executes a task, if for any reason it has to wait for resources to execute the task, this wait, along with the reason for the delay, is recorded by SQL Server. The recording of a wait in SQL Server is known as a **wait stat**. SQL Server tracks many types of wait stats, which we can analyze to understand the reason a task was delayed and perhaps eliminate some needless waits for SQL Server.

Query Execution Life Cycle

Many times in movies or on TV, we see someone in a hurry who experiences difficulty or delay while hailing (signaling for) a taxi. So precious is an available taxi that oftentimes comedies show us two strangers hopping into a taxi simultaneously, each insisting that this is his or her taxi and the other person should get out. If you have just 15 minutes to get to your meeting and it's a 12 minute drive, you have 3 minutes or less to find a taxi. You run the risk of being late, if it takes more than 3 minutes of wait time to signal for and begin your ride. Remember this little story later, because we will frequently use the term "Signal Wait Time" in our discussion of wait stats.

Let's use another taxi example to introduce two additional terms. Suppose that two friends, Tom and Danny, have gone to the mall together. When they leave the mall, they decide to take a taxi. Tom and Danny stand in line waiting for their turn to get into a taxi. This time in line is their "Signal Wait Time" as they are ready to get into a taxi, but the taxis are currently serving other customers. In other words, they are ready but have to wait for their turn. In SQL Server terms, they are in a "runnable state" but are not yet in a "running state."

Now when it is their turn to get into the taxi, the driver informs them he does not take credit cards and can only accept cash. Neither Tom nor Danny has enough cash and thus are not allowed into the vehicle. With no cash in hand, Tom and Danny are no longer in line; they are now in a "suspended state" (known as Query Wait Time in SQL Server). Tom waits while Danny goes to the ATM to fetch the cash. During this time the taxi drivers help other ready (runnable) customers.

Once Danny gets the cash, they are both standing in line again in a runnable state (creating one more Signal Wait Time). When their turn comes this time, they can pay the taxi driver in cash (getting into a "running" state) and are on their way to reaching their destination. The actual travel time taken for the taxi to get from the mall to the destination is the running time (SQL Server calls this CPU Time). It's important to recognize that CPU Time is only part of a query's execution time. In simple words, Query Execution Time is a combination of the following:

CPU Time (Running)
+
Query Wait Time (Suspended State)
+
Signal Wait Time (Runnable)
=
Query Execution Time

In our example, we saw that this task went into all these states at least one time and in some cases multiple times. The order in which our storyline entered each state is detailed below:

Runnable –Tom and Danny, cashless, waiting for a taxi.
Suspended – Tom and Danny not in line (headed to the ATM).
Runnable - Tom and Danny, with cash, waiting for taxi.
Running – Tom and Danny paid the taxi and are leaving the mall.

The Tom and Danny taxi task (leaving the mall) created two runnable states at two different times during one execution. Next time Tom and Danny will probably carry cash to reduce the extra runnable or suspended states. To summarize the three important milestones of the query life-cycle, here are the terms with their definitions:

Running - A query which is being executed on a CPU is called a running query. The length of time in this state is the CPU Time.

Runnable – A query which is ready to execute and waiting for resources is called a runnable query. (In other words, the query is ready to run but the CPU is servicing another query). The amount of time in this state is the Signal Wait Time).

Suspended – A query which is waiting, for any reason, to be converted to runnable, is a suspended query. The time spent in this state is the Query Wait Time. (This is the wait time we are trying to reduce).

Kept Wait Stats

If you had a flurry of wait stats an hour ago and many times throughout the day, it's possible that things in SQL will have already calmed down when you show up to investigate. You might think you have to wait for it to act up again to catch what is going on. The good news is that the SQL Server service has captured the wait stats "kept wait stats" and can show them to you in the sys.dm_os_wait_stats Dynamic Management View (DMV). In Figure 1.1 below, it looks like my SQL Server is tracking 490 different wait types.

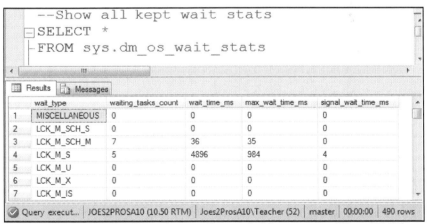

Figure 1.1 The **sys.dm_os_wait_stats Dynamic Management View** (DMV) shows cumulative wait stats information.

Chapter 1. Introduction to Wait Stats

This script uses the dynamic management view (DMV) called sys.dm_os_wait_stats to collect the wait stats. This dynamic management view collects all the information since the time when the SQL Server services have been restarted. We will need to understand how to read what this DMV is telling us about its data.

Let's use another real-life example. If Danny waited 3 seconds for a taxi (3000ms) one day and the next day he waited for a taxi for 2 seconds, it means he has spent 5 seconds of his life waiting for a taxi. Let's also say that Danny has never been on a train. It would be safe to say he has never waited for a train. If Danny has never waited for a train, then he has spent 0 seconds with that wait stat. His overall wait stats look like this:

Wait Type	Wait Time ms
Taxi_Wait	5000
Train_Wait	0

Many of our wait stats have zero milliseconds (wait_time_ms) which means there has been no such stat on that type of wait. Of the 490 possible wait types in SQL Server, which of them has really encountered a wait on your system? By making a slight modification to the earlier query, we can narrow this down to waits we have encountered. Figure 1.2 shows wait times that are over 0 ms (milliseconds).

```
--Show items with some wait time
SELECT *
FROM sys.dm_os_wait_stats
WHERE wait_time_ms > 0
```

	wait_type	waiting_tasks_count	wait_time_ms	max_wait_time_ms	signal_wait_time_ms
1	LCK_M_SCH_M	7	36	35	0
2	LCK_M_S	5	4896	984	4
3	PAGEIOLATCH_SH	997	28675	2057	1367
4	PAGEIOLATCH_UP	48	120	90	67
5	PAGEIOLATCH_EX	5	12	11	0
6	LAZYWRITER_S...	2571	2535752	1242	387

Query executed successfully.　　　　JOES2PROSA10 (10.50 RTM)　Joes2ProsA10\Teach

Figure 1.2 Only 67 wait types have been experienced on this SQL Server since the counters were reset.

Chapter 1. Introduction to Wait Stats

The SELECT statement in Figure 1.2 shows us 5 columns. Here is a quick explanation of each of the columns:

> **wait_type** – This is the name of the wait type. There can be three different kinds of wait types – resource, queue, and external.

> **waiting_tasks_count** – This incremental counter is a good indication of how frequently the wait is happening. If this number is very high, it is a good indication for us to investigate a particular wait type. It is quite possible that the wait time is considerably low, but the frequency of the wait is much higher.

> **wait_time_ms** – This is total accumulated wait time in milliseconds for any type of wait. This is the total wait time and includes signal_wait_time_ms (runnable) plus CPU Time (running) plus Query Wait Time (suspended). This field will always have a value equal to or greater than the signal_wait_time_ms value.

> **max_wait_time_ms** – This indicates the maximum time ever encountered for that particular wait type. Using this, you can estimate the intensity of the wait type in the past. Again, it is not necessarily the case that this max wait time will occur every time; so do not over-invest your effort here.

> **signal_wait_time_ms** – This is the time a thread spends marked as runnable, before it gets to the running state. If the runnable queue is very long, you will find that this wait time becomes high.

Many wait stats are related to one another. The statement in Figure 1.3 shows us three columns. By sorting on wait_time_ms in descending order, the biggest waits come to the top. When the CPU pressure is high, all the CPU-related wait stats appear on top.

But when that CPU pressure is fixed, the wait stats related to the CPU begin showing reasonable percentages.

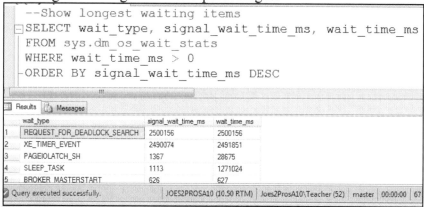

Figure 1.3 The waits with the greatest amount of time are sorted to the top of this query.

Many of the waits in Figure 1.3 are system related, and we generally don't want to look at those stats. The query in Figure 1.4 omits the system-related wait stats, which are not useful to diagnosing performance-related bottlenecks.

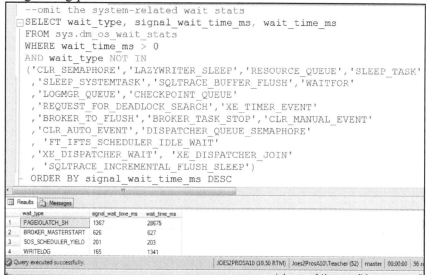

Figure 1.4 The system related wait stats are omitted from this query.

Let's consider another taxi example to really see how this concept comes to life. If the average trip from the airport to the various hotels was about 14 minutes, and the time it took to signal for a taxi was just 1 minute, that would mean one 1/15th of the time (about 7%) you are in a runnable state. About 93% of your time (14 out of 15 minutes), you are in a running state.

The example of 1 minute waiting and 14 running would indicate very little waiting time. In your system, how long are tasks waiting and ready (runnable) compared to how much time they are indeed making headway (running) or in a suspended state. The query in Figure 1.5 shows that tasks are waiting in a runnable state less than 3% of the time.

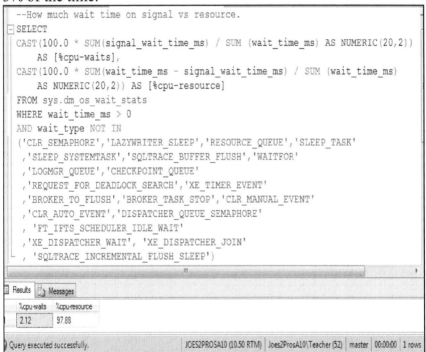

```
--How much wait time on signal vs resource.
SELECT
CAST(100.0 * SUM(signal_wait_time_ms) / SUM (wait_time_ms) AS NUMERIC(20,2))
    AS [%cpu-waits],
CAST(100.0 * SUM(wait_time_ms - signal_wait_time_ms) / SUM (wait_time_ms)
    AS NUMERIC(20,2)) AS [%cpu-resource]
FROM sys.dm_os_wait_stats
WHERE wait_time_ms > 0
AND wait_type NOT IN
('CLR_SEMAPHORE','LAZYWRITER_SLEEP','RESOURCE_QUEUE','SLEEP_TASK'
,'SLEEP_SYSTEMTASK','SQLTRACE_BUFFER_FLUSH','WAITFOR'
,'LOGMGR_QUEUE','CHECKPOINT_QUEUE'
,'REQUEST_FOR_DEADLOCK_SEARCH','XE_TIMER_EVENT'
,'BROKER_TO_FLUSH','BROKER_TASK_STOP','CLR_MANUAL_EVENT'
,'CLR_AUTO_EVENT','DISPATCHER_QUEUE_SEMAPHORE'
, 'FT_IFTS_SCHEDULER_IDLE_WAIT'
,'XE_DISPATCHER_WAIT', 'XE_DISPATCHER_JOIN'
, 'SQLTRACE_INCREMENTAL_FLUSH_SLEEP')
```

%cpu-waits	%cpu-resource
2.12	97.88

Query executed successfully.   JOES2PROSA10 (10.50 RTM) Joes2ProsA10\Teacher (52) master 00:00:00 1 rows

Figure 1.5 Only 2.12% of our query processing time is caused by a signal wait. 97.88% of the time is spent on running the query and/or in a suspended state.

A higher percentage of signal wait stats is not a good indication for the system. A very high value often indicates CPU pressure. In my experience, when systems are running smoothly (and without any glitches) the signal wait stat is lower than 20%. Again, this number can be debated (and it is from my experience and is not documented anywhere). In other words, lower is better and higher is not considered good.

This dynamic management view collects all the information since the time when the SQL Server service has been restarted. This is a cumulative view of the all the wait stats since the last server instance restart. If you have a live production system, you will almost never want to restart your SQL service just to reset some counters. You may want to clear the wait stats manually without restarting your SQL service. You can (at any time) clear all wait stats using the following command:

```
DBCC SQLPERF('sys.dm_os_wait_stats', CLEAR);
```

Summary

The key dynamic management view (DMV), sys.dm_os_wait_stats, helps us to understand our wait stats. This DMV gives us all the information that we need to know regarding wait stats. However, the interpretation is left to us. This is a challenge, as understanding wait stats can often be quite tricky at first. Chapter 3 and beyond will focus more on specializing in the most important wait stats you will need to know.

Introduction to Wait Stats - Points to Ponder

1. A wait stat happens when SQL Server wants to execute a task and it has to wait for resources to execute the task.

2. A task can be in one of three states:
- o Suspended
- o Runnable
- o Running

3. The key dynamic management view (DMV) that helps us to understand wait stats is sys.dm_os_wait_stats.

4. To reset the wait stats in sys.dm_os_wait_stats DMV following use the command
- o DBCC SQLPERF('sys.dm_os_wait_stats', CLEAR);

Acknowledgement

Scripts used in this chapter are inspired from original script written by Glenn Berry. Glenn Berry is an expert in Dynamic Management Views (DMV) and blogs at
http://sqlserverperformance.wordpress.com/

Chapter One - Review Quiz

1) Which of the following is not a status of a wait stat?

    O a. Suspended
    O b. Ran
    O c. Runnable
    O d. Running

2) What is the name of the DMV that helps us to see what wait stats have cumulated on our system?

    O a. sys.dm_os_wait_stats
    O b. sys.dm_os_waiting_tasks

3) One way to reset the cumulative wait stats stored in your system is to restart the SQL Server service. What is another way?

    O a. DBCC SQLPERF('sys.dm_os_wait_stats');
    O b. DBCC SQLPERF('sys.dm_os_wait_stats', RESET);
    O c. DBCC SQLPERF('sys.dm_os_wait_stats', 0);
    O d. DBCC SQLPERF('sys.dm_os_wait_stats', CLEAR);

4) When a task is waiting for a SQL Server resource, what state is it in?

    O a. Suspended
    O b. Ran
    O c. Runnable
    O d. Running

Answer Key

1.) Because Suspended, Runnable, and Running are all states a task can be in, (a) Suspended, (c) Runnable and (d) Running are all wrong. Since Ran is not one of them, (b) is the correct answer.

2.) Because sys.dm_os_waiting_tasks (b) only shows you what is waiting right now (not the history of waits), this makes (b) wrong. We will demonstrate both DMVs later in this book. The sys.dm_os_wait_stats DMV shows a cumulative history, making (a) the correct answer.

3.) Because DBCC SQLPERF requires 2 parameters, (a) is wrong. The correct second parameter is CLEAR, making (b) and (c) wrong. Since (d) uses the CLEAR value for the second parameter, it is the correct choice.

4.) Suspended means the task is not yet ready to run, making (a) incorrect. Ran is not a state, so (b) is wrong. Running means it's not waiting but underway, which is why (d) is not correct. Since Runnable means the task is ready but waiting, (c) is the correct answer.

Chapter 2.   Querying Wait Stats

If a doctor gives you medicine and tells you to come back next week for a checkup, what do you think her main question will be when you come back? She already knows how you felt when you came in before. Now she will want to know how you feel today. If you say you have spent 75% of the last month (3 of the last 4 weeks) feeling ill, it doesn't answer her question about how you feel today.

If you feel good every day for the next month, then that number (% sick time) for the last two months will fall to below 50%. In other words, you are sick only 3 out of 8 weeks, or 37.5 percent of the time, now. If time goes by and you continue to feel well, your average % sick time will drop.

Over time the numbers will smooth out to match what is going on the most often. If you fix something today, then the averages will change eventually. In the stock market they call that a moving average. You may want to know how things are running right at this very moment, and not look at a long history, or wait a long time for averages to start telling the truth.

SQLAuthority.com
Joes2Pros.com

Wait Stats DMVs

Quite often we want to know about the processes running on our server at this given moment in time. We may want to analyze the queries that are currently running, or ones which have recently ran and their plans are still in the cache.

We already learned that the DMV (Dynamic Management View) of sys.dm_os_wait_stats shows cumulative stats are useful when we are looking at an instance-level picture. Sometimes you will want to forget the past and live now and into the future, for SQL wait stats to forget the cumulative past, and try to see what is happening right now.

What is a blocking session? If Jason is updating a table and has it locked, and you want to run a query, you have to wait until Jason is done. The sys.dm_os_waiting_tasks DMV shows all sessions that are currently waiting and the type of resource they are waiting on. Jason has an update that is blocking you, so his update is your blocking session. If a session is waiting on a lock, then the blocking_session_id column (of the sys.dm_os_waiiting_tasks result set) will have the session_id of the lock.

```
SELECT *
FROM sys.dm_os_waiting_tasks
```

waiting_task_address	session_id	exec_context...	wait_duration_...	wait_type	blocking_session_id
0x005AA388	3	0	4494710	XE_DISPATCHER_WAIT	NULL
0x005AA550	4	0	623	LAZYWRITER_SLEEP	NULL
0x005AA718	6	0	4370	REQUEST_FOR_DEADLOCK ...	NULL

Figure 2.1 The sys.dm_os_waiting_tasks DMV shows all currently running session wait stats.

The sys.dm_exec_requests DMV shows each connection to the given instance of SQL Server. Figure 2.2 shows a query of the sys.dm_exec_requests DMV. It will show both user connection tasks and internal connection tasks running in the background. It also has one very valuable field for drilling down, called the sql_handle. The sql_handle points to the memory space of the actual SQL code being used by the task.

```
SELECT *
FROM sys.dm_exec_requests
```

	session_id	request_id	start_time	status	command	sql_handle	statement_start_offset	statement
1	1	0	2011-05-08 14:46:30.710	background	RESOURCE MONITOR	NULL	NULL	NULL
2	2	0	2011-05-08 14:46:30.710	background	XE TIMER	NULL	NULL	NULL
3	3	0	2011-05-08 14:46:30.710	background	XE DISPATCHER	NULL	NULL	NULL
4	4	0	2011-05-08 14:46:30.710	background	LAZY WRITER	NULL	NULL	NULL
5	5	0	2011-05-08 14:46:30.710	background	LOG WRITER	NULL	NULL	NULL

Figure 2.2 The sys.dm_exec_requests DMV shows each connections wait stats.

In Figure 2.2 we can't see our two most important fields at once and we also have many fields we don't care about seeing. To fix this, we can narrow our field select list to just what we want to see. Figure 2.3 shows just the session_id and the sql_handle fields from the sys.dm_exec_requests DMV. *Note:* Since sql_handle is a field and also a reserved keyword, we have enclosed it in brackets.

```
SELECT session_id, [sql_handle]
FROM sys.dm_exec_requests
```

	session_id	sql_handle
1	1	NULL
2	2	NULL
3	3	NULL

Figure 2.3 Just the session_id, and sql_handle fields are shown.

For our next example, we want to see the actual SQL code and will only look at records that have values in the sql_handle field. In

Figure 2.4 we find this by running a query in which the sql_handle does not have any null values.

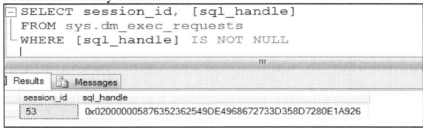

Figure 2.4 One record from the sys.dm_exec_requests DMV has a populated sql_handle value.

As we mentioned earlier, the sys.dm_exec_requests DMV offers something that the sys.dm_os_waiting_tasks does not. One of the fields is called sql_handle, which is a binary key value. You can use this to retrieve queries from the procedure cache.

How do you use the data in the sql_handle field? We will show you that trick very soon. For now let's join the sys.dm_exec_requests DMV to the sys.dm_os_waiting_tasks DMV. We will get the session_id from the sys.dm_os_waiting_tasks DMV and the sql_handle from the sys.dm_exec_requests DMV. *Note:* If your session (in this case 54) has finished running, then you would have no waiting tasks and may not get any records in this query.

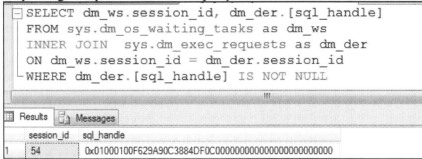

Figure 2.5 Getting the session_id and the sql_handle by joining the sys.dm_exec_requests DMV to the sys.dm_os_waiting_tasks DMV.

Wait Stats DMFs

The sys.dm_exec_sql_text Dynamic Management Function (DMF) will return a result set of 1 record for each valid sql_handle you feed into it. Figure 2.6 shows the code that is saved in the memory space that the sql_handle points to. It looks like we found a CREATE DATABASE statement that currently has wait stats. You can see this in the text field of the sys.dm_exec_sql_text DMF (Dynamic Management Function). In Figure 2.6, this is the field furthest to the right.

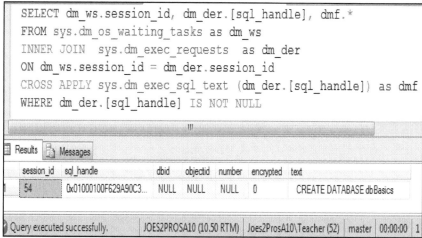

Figure 2.6 Using a CROSS APPLY with the sys.dm_exec_sql_text function shows the code running inside the memory pointed to by the sql_handle.

To correlate related records from a table and a table valued function, we use the CROSS APPLY. The CROSS APPLY acts very similar to an INNER JOIN but works between results sets that require parameters instead of an ON clause to combine the records.

This example assumes the reader knows how to use the advanced query technique, CROSS APPLY. The short description of what it does is that it acts like an INNER JOIN between a table and a

function that returns a result set. A parameterized table-valued
function returns rows and columns just like a table. Unfortunately
you can't join a parameterized table valued function to table. For a
more extensive lesson on using CROSS APPLY, please see
Chapter 12 of *SQL Queries Joes 2 Pros*: (ISBN 1-4392-5318-8).

This query against the DMVs and the DMFs is written taking this
into consideration: we want to analyze the queries that are
currently running, or which have recently run, and their plans are
still in the cache.

```
SELECT dm_ws.wait_duration_ms,
dm_ws.wait_type,
dm_es.status,
dm_t.[TEXT],
dm_ws.session_ID,
dm_es.cpu_time,
dm_es.memory_usage,
dm_es.logical_reads,
dm_es.total_elapsed_time,
dm_es.program_name,
DB_NAME(dm_r.database_id) DatabaseName,
-- Optional columns
dm_ws.blocking_session_id,
dm_r.wait_resource,
dm_es.login_name,
dm_r.command,
dm_r.last_wait_type
FROM sys.dm_os_waiting_tasks dm_ws
INNER JOIN sys.dm_exec_requests dm_r ON dm_ws.session_id = dm_r.session_id
INNER JOIN sys.dm_exec_sessions dm_es ON dm_es.session_id = dm_r.session_id
CROSS APPLY sys.dm_exec_sql_text (dm_r.sql_handle) dm_t
WHERE dm_es.is_user_process = 1
```

	wait_duration_ms	wait_type	status	TEXT	session_ID	cpu_time	memory_usage	logical_reads	total_ela
1	16	IO_COMPLETION	running	CREATE DATABASE dbBasics	54	1980	2	41281	16958

Figure 2.7 Limiting the field select list to many of the most used user processes
(WHERE cm_es.is_user_process = 1).

Let's analyze the result of the above query and see how it can be
helpful in identifying the blocking query, and the kind of wait

types it has created. The above query will return various columns. The various columns that provide very important details are explained below:

> **wait_duration_ms** – Indicates the current wait time for the query that is executing at that point in time.
>
> **wait_type** – Indicates the current wait type for the query.
>
> **TEXT** – Indicates the query text.

There are many other important pieces of information, like cpu_time, memory_usage, and logical_reads, which can be read from the query as well. You can pick all the fields or just the ones that matter most to you.

Persisting Wait Stat Data

If you have ever seen a "Makeover" show, then odds are you have seen many "before and after" examples. A commercial about hair gel will often show what the same person looked like before (on the left side of the TV), and how they look afterwards (on the right side of the TV). You often see this with weight loss programs like "The Biggest Loser". We are amazed at the improvement even more when we see both pictures at once. Without the "before" picture, it would be hard to tell how much things have improved.

That "before" picture is your baseline. A baseline is a measure of how things were going before you made any changes. Baselining is the verb "to create a baseline". In other words, it is simply taking the action to record your baseline, so you can later take another measurement to know how much your actions have helped.

Once you fix a problem, your average wait times will likely come down. Let's say your fix took place an hour ago. If you had this problem for 23 of the last 24 hours, then the cumulative nature of the sys.dm_os_wait_stats DMV will show negligible improvement stats thanks to the last hour running better.

It would be useful to see what has happened in the last hour after the fix and compare that to your baseline of the hour of activity before the fix. Before we get too far, remember this means instead of one big cumulative dataset we will need two sets of data. SQL normally does not hold two similar sets of the same type of data. You can do this with two tables or put two sets of data in one table. If want to put your baseline results and test results into the same table, make sure to flag the records activity. With that in mind, here are some points that we had covered earlier about resetting the cumulative wait stats in the sys.dm_os_wait_stats DMV:

1. Wait stats are reset when the SQL Server service is restarted.

2. Wait stats can be reset manually with a DBCC statement.

Sometimes performance tuning experts make modifications to the server and try to measure the wait stats for a given duration. This report needs to capture the baseline data as well as the operational data after the changes were made.

Think of semester grades at a school. Let's say you had one bad semester last year, but you worked really hard this year and got all "A" grades. If you got "C" grades last year and did "A" work this year, it would be a shame if the teacher was still counting last year's papers and tests into this year's grades. Yes, all the work you are doing this year should persist, but none of last year's work should be in consideration.

It would also be a bad situation if you scored in the high 90s all year long and got an 89 on the final. Your overall average should pull you through just fine, unless the teacher says she lost all your work and only remembers the last thing you did, which was the 89 score.

You can see that there is a need for making the right batch of data persistent, so that we can take a look at it later for our comparison. If you are going to test and compare one hour against the next, make sure you get all stats bunched together in the right way. We will flag all baseline activity with a 1 and all post-change activity with a 2. Use the following steps as an example of how to measure the wait stats over the time:

1. Reset the wait stats.
2. Run for one hour and record to a table (flag as 1).
3. Make your changes or fixes to SQL Server.
4. Reset the wait stats.
5. Run for one hour and record to a table (flag as 2).

To capture the results from sys.dm_os_wait_stats DMV, we need a table that captures many of the same fields as the DMV. In Figure 2.8, we create the MyWaitStatTable to hold data from the sys.dm_os_wait_stats DMV.

```
SQLQuery1.sql - J...10\Teacher (52))*
   -- Create Persisted Wait Stats Table
   CREATE TABLE [MyWaitStatTable](
   [wait_type] [nvarchar](60) NOT NULL,
   [waiting_tasks_count] [bigint] NOT NULL,
   [wait_time_ms] [bigint] NOT NULL,
   [max_wait_time_ms] [bigint] NOT NULL,
   [signal_wait_time_ms] [bigint] NOT NULL,
   [CurrentDateTime] DATETIME NOT NULL,
   [Flag] INT
   )
   GO
```

```
Messages
Command(s) completed successfully.
```

Figure 2.8 The MyWaitStatTable is created to capture records from the sys.dm_os_wait_stats DMV.

We need to clear our cumulative history from sys.dm_os_wait_stats DMV and start our baseline recording. In Figure 2.9 we use the DBCC command to clear the records.

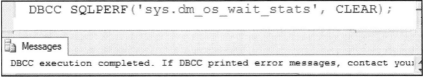

```
   DBCC SQLPERF('sys.dm_os_wait_stats', CLEAR);
```

```
Messages
DBCC execution completed. If DBCC printed error messages, contact you
```

Figure 2.9 The sys.dm_os_wait_stats DMV records are reset.

After we run for a set period of time (in this case one hour), we need to capture the results into MyWaitStatTable. Figure 2.10 shows an insert statement that captures all existing records from the sys.dm_os_wait_stats DMV and marks them as a baseline (Flag 1).

```
-- Populate Table for 1 hour before (Flag 1)
INSERT INTO MyWaitStatTable
([wait_type],
[waiting_tasks_count],
[wait_time_ms],
[max_wait_time_ms],
[signal_wait_time_ms],
[CurrentDateTime],
[Flag])
    SELECT
    [wait_type],
    [waiting_tasks_count],
    [wait_time_ms],
    [max_wait_time_ms],
    [signal_wait_time_ms],
    GETDATE(), 1 --Flag 1 means Baseline
    FROM sys.dm_os_wait_stats
        GO
```

Figure 2.10 After 1 hour of baselining, we capture the records from the sys.dm_os_wait_stats DMV to MyWaitStatTable.

Now that your baseline data has been persisted to the MyWaitStatsTable, we are ready for the next step. Make the changes or fixes to your SQL Server, and be sure to clear out all the records.

As of now the older, baseline measurements you already captured into MyWaitStatsTable are also in the DMV. You need to start collecting new information with a fresh slate. You might remember that to clear the records without restarting SQL Server use the DBCC SQLPERF statement. By clearing the DMV, you are ready to start recording new data. After you make those system fixes to tune your SQL Server, it's time to run the code you did before (shown earlier in Figure 2.9).

36

Your next step is to keep your normal server operations running under the new configuration. After the same amount of time goes by (in our example 1 hour), populate the table with flag 2 data (post-change). Figure 2.11 is similar to 2.10 except we have changed the flag value to 2.

```
    -- Populate Table for 1 hour before (Flag 1)
INSERT INTO MyWaitStatTable
([wait_type],
[waiting_tasks_count],
[wait_time_ms],
[max_wait_time_ms],
[signal_wait_time_ms],
[CurrentDateTime],
[Flag])
    SELECT
    [wait_type],
    [waiting_tasks_count],
    [wait_time_ms],
    [max_wait_time_ms],
    [signal_wait_time_ms],
    GETDATE(), 2 --Flag 2 means 2nd State
    FROM sys.dm_os_wait_stats
    GO
```

Messages

Command(s) completed successfully.

Figure 2.11 For 1 hour after your change baselining capture the records from the sys.dm_os_wait_stats DMV to the MyWaitStatTable.

Now to see our famous before and after results. By doing a self join on MyWaitStatTable, you can compare the two groups of data (baseline and post-change). Many things probably got better. Did anything get worse? Yikes, my system got worse on 2 wait stats. The example in Figure 2.12 shows my waits times actually went up. In this case we say it got worse, since the Later_WaitTime expression field has a higher value than the Original_WaitTime field.

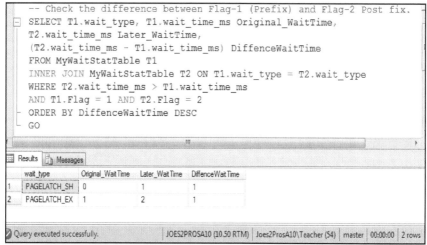

Figure 2.12 A self join on MyWaitStatTable shows the comparison of waits before and after your changes.

We used the additional column (called flag) to capture the wait stats. We used it in the SELECT query to see the wait stats related to that time group. We used just 2 groups (baseline and 1 post-change). Many times, I select more than five or six different sets of wait stats, and I find this method of flagging each test phase very convenient in finding the difference between wait stats.

Querying Wait Stats - Points to Ponder

1. If a session is waiting on a lock, then the blocking_session_id column of the sys.dm_os_waiting_tasks DMV will have the session_id of the lock.

2. The sql_handle of the sys.dm_exec_requests DMV points to the memory space of the actual SQL code being used by the task

3. You can get the SQL code from the sys.dm_exec_sql_text Dynamic Management Function (DMF) by passing in the SQL handle

4. To correlate records from a table and a table valued function, use CROSS APPLY

5. A baseline is a measure of how things were going before you made any changes.

6. Use the following steps as an example of how to measure the wait stats over time:

   o Reset the wait stats.

   o Run for one hour and record to a table (flag as 1).

   o Make your changes or fixes to SQL Server.

   o Reset the wait stats.

   o Run for one hour and record to a table (flag as 2).

7. Run the DBCC SQLPERF('sys.dm_os_wait_stats', CLEAR) statement to clear the history from the sys.dm_os_wait_stats DMV and start baseline recording.

Chapter Two - Review Quiz

1) Which are 2 DMVs that relate to viewing all types of Wait Stats (Choose Two)?

    □ a. sys.dm_os_wait_stats
    □ b. sys.dm_os_waiting_tasks
    □ c. dm_db_partition_stats
    □ d. dm_exec_procedure_stats

2) What is the name of the DMV that helps us to see which Wait Stats are active on your system at the present time?

    O a. sys.dm_os_wait_stats
    O b. sys.dm_os_waiting_tasks

3) The value of the Waiting_Task_Address in the sys.dm_os_waiting_tasks DMV contains what type of data?

    O a. SPID
    O b. Memory Address
    O c. T-SQL Text

4) What happens to a Runnable Task in the sys.dm_os_waiting_tasks DMV when it turns to a running task?

    O a. The Status Changes in the DMV.
    O b. The record disappears from the DMV.

5) When used with the sys.dm_os_waiting_tasks DMV, how does the sys.dm_exec_sql_text DMF help in diagnosing waits?

    O a. The sys.dm_exec_sql_text DMF will show you the T-SQL Text of the blocking session.
    O b. The sys.dm_exec_sql_text DMF will show you how many times the same record in the DMV was blocked.

Answer Key

1.) The only DMVs that are able to view any type of Wait Stat have the word "Wait" in the name, this makes (c) and (d) incorrect. Therefore, (a) and (b) are the correct answers.

2.) Because sys.dm_os_wait_stats (a) shows you all past and present wait stats, this makes (a) wrong. This means sys.dm_os_waiting_tasks (b) is the correct answer.

3.) Because Waiting_Task_Address points to a location in memory in Hex form, and (a) and (c) contain base-10 numbers, those choices are wrong. The correct answer is the memory address, making (b) the correct choice.

4.) The sys.dm_os_waiting_tasks DMV only shows waiting tasks, which makes (a) incorrect. Since runnable means waiting, and only waiting (runnable) tasks are listed in the sys.dm_os_waiting_tasks DMV, (b) is the correct answer.

5.) The sys.dm_exec_sql_text can take a memory address space and show you the SQL code. It will not show any history, making (b) incorrect. Since it shows the SQL code, (a) is the correct answer.

Chapter 3. Parallel Execution

After renting a moving truck for a single day, my friend, Bobby, realized he could not move all his belongings by himself. He needed some help and asked me to be a second resource. Together we were able to get this one task done in one full day. He knew there was no chance the work could have been done on time, had he attempted the move by himself.

In the everyday world, we call it "teamwork" when many individuals work in parallel. In the computing world, this concept is known as "parallel execution." The ability to apply additional resources to a single big task to accomplish it more efficiently is the chief benefit of parallel execution.

However, when using multiple resources to more quickly accomplish tasks, you need coordination to manage the workload. In this chapter we cover wait stats which can arise from parallel execution.

CXPACKET

CXPACKET is one of the most popular wait stats. I have commonly seen CXPACKET appear as one of the top five wait stats in most systems having more than one CPU.

The purpose of parallel execution is to accomplish a task faster. Parallel operations include multiple threads for a single query. For example, two threads searching through 5,000 records would run faster than one thread searching all 10,000. Each query deals with a different set of the data (or rows). Even if you split the work evenly, one thread would finish slightly ahead of the other thread.

Note that not all CXPACKET wait types are bad. Imagine you hired two people to work in your yard and at the end of the day you cordially decided to share a special dinner inside your home for them. When you call them in for dinner, they stop working, put their tools away, and head towards the door you hold open for them. Before they can come in the house, they both must remove their shoes. The worker who gets his shoes off first will walk through the door you are holding open. Being polite, you continue to hold the door open until the second worker comes in, which takes about five seconds. These five seconds where you hold the door is similar to CXPACKET's wait. You can think of the extra five seconds (i.e., waiting for the last shoe to come off) as wasted time, but you saved much more time overall by having two days' work done in a single day.

When one or more of the threads lags behind, the CXPACKET wait stat is created. There is an organizer-coordinator thread (thread 0), which waits for all the worker threads to complete. Thread 0 is holding the door (so to speak) for the worker threads. This coordinator thread gathers results and presents them on the client side. The organizer thread has to wait for the all the worker threads to finish before it can mark the work as complete and move ahead. The wait by this organizer thread from the time the first thread is done until the last thread is done is called the CXPACKET wait.

We have all experienced cases when a small wait makes good sense for the benefit of teamwork. There may also be cases when a wait is unavoidable (e.g., in cases where workers on a project will not all finish their respective tasks at exactly the same time). If you remove this particular wait type for any query, then that query may run slower because parallel operations would be disabled. If you determine the wait is longer than the gain of having many worker threads, then you can make a change. You may consider lowering the degree of parallelism if contention on this wait type becomes a problem.

Database Considerations for CXPACKET

Are your tasks really small? If you only had 10 minutes of work to do in your yard, you would not want the overhead of hiring two people. One worker can do that small job in a very short period of time. In order to ensure that SQL Server doesn't attempt to "hire" additional resources for small jobs, we will use an advanced setting which affects the server workload type and reduces CXPACKET.

On pure OLTP (online transactional processing) systems, where the transactions are smaller and tend to run very quickly, set the "Max Degree of Parallelism" to 1 (one). This way it makes sure that the query never attempts parallelism and does not incur unnecessary resource overhead.

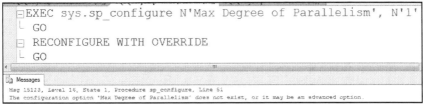

Figure 3.1 the sp_configure system stored procedure has reduced the parallelism to 1.

Before you can run the code in Figure 3.1, please make sure your advanced options for SQL Server are enabled. You can do this using the code you see below (Figure 3.2).

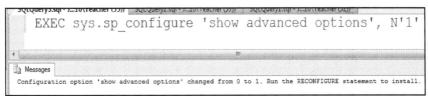

Figure 3.2 You may need to enable advanced options to change your Max Degree of Parallelism.

With the advanced options on, we can set the "Max Degree of Parallelism" option. In Figure 3.3 we set it to 1, which will eliminate the CXPACKET wait stat.

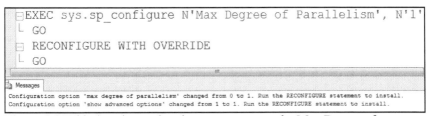

Figure 3.3 With the advanced option on, we can set the Max Degree of Parallelism to 1.

Data-warehousing and reporting systems both tend to have very large tasks and thus benefit greatly from parallelism. Since queries against these OLAP (online analytical processing) systems will be

45

running for a long time, it is advised to set the "Maximum Degree of Parallelism" to 0 (zero), which means unlimited. This way most of the queries will utilize the parallel processor, and long running queries get a boost in their performance due to multiple processors.

CXPACKET Potential Problems

For mixed systems (OLTP + OLAP), there is a challenge where the right balance has to be found. My approach to these is very simple. I set the "Maximum Degree of Parallelism" to 2, which means the query uses parallelism but only on two CPUs. However, I keep the "Cost Threshold for Parallelism" very high. This way, not all the queries will qualify for parallelism but only the queries with higher costs will utilize parallelism. I have found this to work best for a system that has OLTP queries but also has a reporting server.

In Figure 3.4, I am setting 'Cost Threshold for Parallelism' to 25 values (which are just for illustration); you can choose any value, and you can find it out by experimenting with the system. You can also see I am setting the 'Max Degree of Parallelism' to 2, so the query will qualify for parallel querying to run on two (2) CPUs.

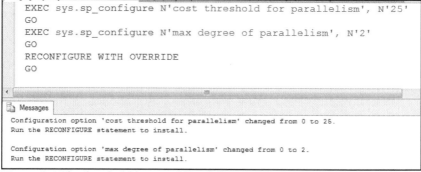

```
EXEC sys.sp_configure N'cost threshold for parallelism', N'25'
GO
EXEC sys.sp_configure N'max degree of parallelism', N'2'
GO
RECONFIGURE WITH OVERRIDE
GO
```

Messages

Configuration option 'cost threshold for parallelism' changed from 0 to 25.
Run the RECONFIGURE statement to install.

Configuration option 'max degree of parallelism' changed from 0 to 2.
Run the RECONFIGURE statement to install.

Figure 3.4 The threshold is set to 25 and the max number of CPUs is set to 2.

Suppose you have a medium-sized query taking 15 seconds to run, but it could be run in 14 seconds, if you created a parallel operation. Would that time savings be worth setting up the cost of parallelism? Probably not. How about if it could take a 50 second query down to 3 seconds? How much savings do you need before you want parallelism to kick in? The 'Cost Threshold for Parallelism' refers to the estimated increased elapsed time in seconds required to execute the serial plan on a specific hardware configuration. The 'Cost Threshold for Parallelism' set to 25 indicates that the query that will need to have a higher cost (here, more than 25 seconds) to qualify for parallelism.

In Figure 3.4, we will allow you to use up to two CPUs for a single task if it will save at least 25 seconds. This implies that, regardless of the number of CPUs, the query will select any two CPUs while executing.

When you use the 'Cost Threshold for Parallelism', SQL Server executes a parallel query plan if the estimated cost is higher. How much higher is up to you. For example, if you know a serial execution (1 CPU) would take 50 seconds and two parallel CPUs would take 35 seconds, is that enough? If you set the threshold to 10 seconds, then this works because the parallel process saves you 15 seconds (50-35=15). If you set the threshold to 25, then the serial execution (being only 15 seconds slower) would still be chosen.

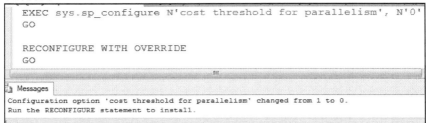

Figure 3.5 Setting the cost threshold to zero allows SQL to choose the cost for parallel execution.

Suppose that things run very well following these two changes. So you close your query window and call it a day. Weeks later, the boss gives you great praise and asks what setting you used so they can do the same thing on other similar servers within the company. You know you set the 'Cost Threshold for Parallelism' and the 'Max Degree of Parallelism' setting, but you can't remember the numbers.

We know the parallelism has been set back to 0. Let's set it back to 2 with the following code:

EXEC sys.sp_configure N'Cost threshold for parallelism',N'2'
GO
RECONFIGURE WITH OVERRIDE
GO

How can you now check to see what this setting is? You can locate these details by navigating to Server Properties and looking at the Advanced page (as shown in Figure 3.6). We see the 'Cost Threshold for Parallelism' is set to 25 and the 'Max Degree of Parallelism' is set to 2.

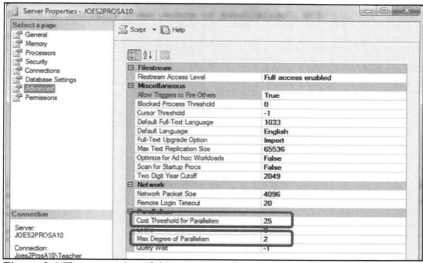

Figure 3.6 The properties of the server confirm the threshold is 25 and the max parallelism is 2.

Reducing CXPACKET

You will have little to no CXPACKET wait stats with well balanced parallelism or a simple single CPU serial operation. Returning to the garden example, why might one of your two workers finish his half of the yard in four hours while another takes six hours to complete? Perhaps you split the yard in two sections and one worker got the section with all the heavy rocks or big weeds.

The end result is that one worker finishes two hours ahead of the other. You don't want to hold the door open for two hours, so you try your best to split the work evenly. The following reasons are often the major cause of CXPACKET wait time and can cause excessive unnecessary waiting:

1. Data which is heavily skewed in variable data type fields (e.g., some rows have 60 bytes and others can be over 500 bytes). This can easily lead to uneven workload on threads and thus may create CXPACKET wait.

2. While retrieving the data, if one of the threads faces IO, Memory, or CPU bottleneck, then it will have to wait for those resources in order to execute its tasks.

3. If needed data must be retrieved from a resource having a different IO Subsystem speed, this can incur long waits. (This is a rare but possible scenario).

4. Higher fragmentations in some areas of the table can lead to less data per page and thus require added IO cycles to retrieve data.

Best Practices for CXPACKET

So if parallel execution gets off balance, the wait for the last CPU can become too high. How do you balance everything out? Here are a few best practices:

49

1. De-fragmentation of indexes can help, since more data per page can be obtained. (Assuming close to 100% fill-factor.)

2. An even workload split across a slow drive and a fast drive will mean one drive must wait while the other finishes. If your data is on multiple data files across multiple physical disks, ensuring that the physical drives have similar speed may reduce the CXPACKET wait.

3. Updating statistics can significantly improve the ability of the query optimizer to render a better execution plan. Keeping the statistics updated means the query optimizer will have better estimates when assigning threads and dividing the data among available threads.

Bad Practices for CXPACKET

In one of my recent consultancy projects, I noticed that one of the experienced DBA employees observed higher CXPACKET waits and by trying to reduce them, he increased the worker threads. The reality was that increasing worker threads led to many other issues. With a greater number of the threads, more amount of memory was used and pressured the system. As there were more threads, the CPU scheduler faced higher 'Context Switching' and performance was further degraded. When I explained all these to DBA he suggested that now we should reduce the number of threads. Not really! Lowering the number of the threads may create heavy stalling for parallel queries. I suggest not touching the setting of number of the threads when dealing with CXPACKET wait.

Parallel Execution - Points to Ponder

1. Parallel executions are important for computing since it allows more processing power (worker threads) at higher speed to be used for a single task.

2. There is an organizer-coordinator thread (thread 0), which creates organized worker threads into tasks which wait for all the worker threads to complete before the task can be closed.

3. When a big task has multiple threads starting at the same time, they won't always finish at the same time. When one or more of the threads will lag behind, thread 0 has to wait for all threads to finish, thereby creating the CXPACKET wait stat.

4. Note that not all the CXPACKET wait types are bad, since they only exist during parallel execution (i.e., which usually make things run faster).

5. Small tasks should not use multiple worker threads and will run more efficiently with just one thread.

6. Data-warehousing / Reporting servers tend to have very large tasks. They benefit from parallelism and will invariably have some CXPACKET wait types while large projects finish processing.

7. You will have little to no CXPACKET wait time with well-balanced parallelism or simple single CPU serial operation.

8. Mixed systems (OLTP + OLAP) present more of a challenge and the right balance must be found.

9. In order to help SQL Server split tasks evenly, the following items are advised:
     o Ensure that indexes are defragmented.
     o When data is on multiple data files on multiple physical disks, make sure the disks (i.e., the physical drives) are of similar speed.
     o Keep the SQL statistics updated.

10. If you set the 'Max Degree of Parallelism' to 1, there will be no parallel processes and therefore no CXPACKET wait types.

11. Setting the parallelism to 0 (zero) allows SQL to use as much parallel execution as necessary.

12. When you use the 'Cost Threshold for Parallelism' setting, SQL Server executes a parallel query plan when the estimated cost is higher. 'Cost Threshold for Parallelism' refers to the estimated elapsed time in seconds required to execute the serial plan on a specific hardware configuration.

Chapter Three - Review Quiz

1) When does the CXPACKET wait stat occur?
 O a. The worker thread is waiting for coordinator threads.
 O b. The worker coordinator thread is waiting for worker threads.

2) What is the only way to eliminate the CXPACKET wait type?
 O a. Disable parallel execution.
 O b. Set the Cost of Parallelism to a very high value.

3) What type of tasks would more likely use multiple worker threads in parallel?
 O a. Small OLTP tasks.
 O b. Very large data-warehousing.
 O c. All tasks will benefit from parallel executions.
 O d. No tasks will benefit from parallel executions.

4) Setting the 'Cost Threshold for Parallelism' to 5 means what?

O a. Only tasks that execute 5 seconds faster will use parallelism.

O b. All Parallel tasks will use 5 worker threads.

O c. All parallel tasks will use 5 coordinator threads.

O d. The record disappears from the DMV.

Answer Key

1.) The CXPACKET wait stat occurs when the Coordinator thread has to wait for all processes to complete, so (b) is correct. The thread workload is split by the Coordinator thread at the point the process runs, so there is no wait time for this. Answer (a) is wrong.

2.) Disabling parallel execution will eliminate CXPACKET wait types but remember the queries may execute slower. Answer (a) is correct. Setting the cost of parallelism high will not eliminate CXPACKET Wait Types but will increase performance if well balanced. Answer (b) is incorrect.

3.) Parallelism only benefits large tasks that would execute quicker with multiple workers working on the same task, so (b) is correct. Small tasks run very quickly, so you would not see any benefit from parallelism. Answers (a), (c), and (d) are incorrect.

4.) Setting the 'Cost Threshold for Parallelism' only affects the task that will decrease runtime from serial by the set amount (5 seconds) to be executed using parallelism. The correct answer is (a) because setting the 'Cost Threshold' does not affect the number of threads or the number of Coordinator threads.

Chapter 4. Multi-Tasking Waits

Have you ever tried speaking to someone while they are noticeably preoccupied? Perhaps they were reading a book or watching the last few minutes of a big game. You can tell they are able to watch TV and perhaps listen to you, but they cannot do both very well at the same time.

There are other situations where you can easily do two things at once. With our friends on a sunny day we often walk, talk, and breathe as we stroll through the park. The task of walking does not need to stop to allow for the tasks of talking or breathing to take place. All these events can happen simultaneously.

At this point, you probably already know this story is hinting at multi-tasking. There are different types of multi-tasking and since SQL Server works with other systems in your enterprise, sometimes the waits are beyond SQL's direct control.

SOS_SCHEDULER_YIELD

Doctors generally recommend that we consume 6-9 cups of water per day (1.6 liters) for good health. If you are thirsty and see a nice cool drinking fountain, odds are you are not going to consume 1.6 liters at one visit. If you tried, then it would take a long time and the people standing behind you waiting for their drink would get very irritated. After a few quenching ounces you should cooperatively give up your spot and go about your day. You can return to the fountain later. If everyone is courteous, then nobody will be consuming too much while making everyone else become even thirstier while waiting in line for a long time.

Actually a better example is when I was on the metro reading my book. My stop was over 30 minutes away so I might be in the seat for a while. Every seat on the metro was full and at the next stop a pregnant woman and her six year old daughter got on board. The daughter said "how much longer mommy?" She explained that they were 10 minutes from their stop. With every seat full, I voluntarily gave up my seat for the woman. She sat down with her daughter on her lap. While standing and holding the ceiling strap (for my own balance) with one hand, I could not hold my book open to read. Now for me it was idle time and no work was getting done. Instead I looked out the window and enjoyed the passing scenery.

The SOS_SCHEDULER_YIELD occurs when a task voluntarily gives up execution for other tasks to execute. SQL Server has multiple threads to execute multiple tasks at the same time. The basic working methodology for SQL Server is that it does not let any "runnable" thread starve. Now let us assume SQL Server is on an operating system that is very busy running all threads on all the schedulers. There are always new tasks coming up which are ready to run (in other words, runnable). The good news is thread management of the SQL Server service is decided by SQL Server and not the operating system.

SQL has a policy for managing its own threads. SQL Server runs co-operatively and can let other threads run from time to time by having them yield themselves. When any thread yields itself for another thread, it creates this its own wait under some rare peak condition. Sometimes this peak condition is temporary and soon there will be plenty of resource for all tasks.

When there are more waiting threads building up all the time, it clearly indicates that the CPU is under pressure. You can run the sys.dm_os_schedulers DMV to see how many runnable task counts there are in your system. Figure 4.1 shows was have just 1 runnable task which means there is very little waiting on this system.

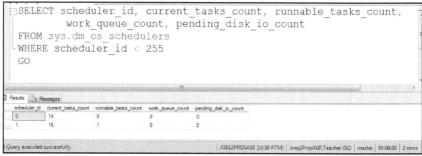

Figure 4.1 A query from the sys.dm_os_schedulers shows how many runnable (waiting tasks) your system has at this point in time.

All schedulers running regular queries have ID numbers less than 1048576. Those schedulers with higher numbers are used internally by SQL Server. Our WHERE clause specifies very low numbers (WHERE scheduler_id <255). It's clear that when lines get longer at the shopping mail, it means the store is not keeping up with the shoppers. If five people are standing in line, that is not nearly as bad as if twelve people are waiting. In SQL Server, if you notice a two-digit number in the runnable_tasks_count field continuously for long time (not once in a while), this indicates CPU pressure. The CPU is not able to keep up with the load. The two-digit number in runnable_tasks_count is generallys a bad thing.

SOS_SCHEDULER_YIELD Potential Problems

Recall my Metro example where all seats were full and more people entered. When there weren't enough seats to handle the demand of every passenger, I voluntarily gave up my seat. My hope was that a seat would free up when other passengers exited. Then my voluntary wait would end and I would be able to sit down and start reading my book.

When you see a high number of waiting (runnable) tasks, you might want to verify whether it is due to processor or memory pressure. You can use Performance Monitor (Perfmon) to help verify this, as well as several other counters (%Processor Time and other processor related counters).

At first people often wonder why a CPU falling behind might be cured by adding more memory. Think of the hardest working person you know filing papers in a big office with a big table full of marked folders. He is getting the job done quickly. The next day you tell him the room is being remodeled and he needs to work on the small corner table in the break room. That same talented worker will get less done and perhaps even fall behind. Memory is like the workspace for a CPU. Providing the right amount can allow a CPU to keep up with work demands.

Reducing SOS_SCHEDULER_YIELD Wait

This is the trickiest part of this procedure. As discussed, this particular wait type relates to CPU pressure. In simple terms, increasing CPU is the solution; however, it is not easy to implement this solution. There are other things that you can consider when this wait type is very high. The query below will search all cached queries and will find the most expensive query in terms of CPU.

Note: Make certain that all queries you wish to evaluate have been cached. A query that uses lots of resources but is not cached will not be detected by this query:

```
SELECT SUBSTRING(qt.TEXT,
(qs.statement_start_offset/2)+1,
((CASE qs.statement_end_offset
WHEN -1 THEN DATALENGTH(qt.TEXT)
ELSE qs.statement_end_offset
END - qs.statement_start_offset)/2)+1),
qs.execution_count,
qs.total_logical_reads,
qs.last_logical_reads,
qs.total_logical_writes,
qs.last_logical_writes,
qs.total_worker_time,
qs.last_worker_time,
qs.total_elapsed_time/1000000
total_elapsed_time_in_S,
qs.last_elapsed_time/1000000
last_elapsed_time_in_S,
qs.last_execution_time,
qp.query_plan
FROM sys.dm_exec_query_stats qs
CROSS APPLY
sys.dm_exec_sql_text(qs.sql_handle) qt
CROSS APPLY
sys.dm_exec_query_plan(qs.plan_handle) qp
ORDER BY qs.total_worker_time DESC -- CPU
time
```

You can find the most expensive queries that are utilizing lots of CPU (from the cache) and tune them accordingly. Moreover, you can find the longest running query and attempt to tune it by checking for any processor offending code.

Additionally, pay attention to total_worker_time, because if that is also consistently higher, then the CPU under too much pressure.

Performance Monitor can store a compilation of measurements over time. You can also check Perfmon counters as compilations, as they tend to use a fair amount of CPU. Index rebuilding is also a CPU intensive process but we should consider that main cause for this query because that is indeed needed on high transactions OLTP system utilized to reduce fragmentations.

Multi-Tasking Types

If any of you are parents of two or more children you know how delightful it is during those moments when your children seem to play well together and cooperate. Laughing and sharing is a delight to see and becomes a memorable moment for your family. A child plays with one toy while the other plays with another toy. Later they swap toys in a form of cooperative sharing. Yes, a very ideal situation that does not always happen and we will discuss the problem side later.

For now, imagine Tommy is playing with the red toy car and his little sister, Sue, wants to use it. She indicates this wish, so Tommy finishes what he is doing and sets the red toy car aside. Sue then plays with it and all is well. Does it go this way in your household all the time? What else might happen on a bad day when Sue asks to play with the red toy car? Tommy might refuse and play with it all evening. Sue could be waiting for hours knowing this cooperative forum is not working for her. Long waits are a result.

At this point Sue more likely will want to shift to a preemptive measure and yell "Mommy". Hearing this scream, Tommy might give up his toy sooner than he had planned since mom would veto his use of the toy.

When things are working well cooperatively, then there is no need to intervene with how tasks work together. I often get questions related to SQL Server 2008 Books-Online about various preemptive wait types. I got a few questions asking what these wait types are and how they should be interpreted. Before we continue discussing them, let's first study what is meant by the terms PREEMPTIVE and Non-PREEMPTIVE waits in SQL Server.

PREEMPTIVE Multi-Tasking

Simply put, this wait is non-cooperative. While SQL Server is executing a task, the operating system (OS) might determine this task is unfairly getting too many resources while other tasks are waiting. The OS interrupts the task and gives the CPU to another task. This leads SQL Server to involuntarily give up the execution for other higher priority tasks. This is not good for SQL Server, as it is an external process which makes SQL Server yield. This kind of wait can drastically reduce performance and should be investigated.

Cooperative (Non-PREEMPTIVE) Multi-Tasking

In simple terms, this wait is cooperative. SQL Server manages the scheduling of the threads. When SQL Server manages the scheduling instead of the OS, it determines its own priority. In this case, SQL Server sets the priority and one thread yields to another thread voluntarily based upon priority.

Both Types of Multi-Tasking in SQL

SQL Server's default is non-preemptive mode, which works fine most of the time. Conversely when CLR, extended stored procedures, and other external components run in SQL, they run in Preemptive mode. These tasks lead to the creation of preemptive wait types.

In the earlier versions of SQL Server, there were no preemptive wait types mentioned and the associated task status was marked as "suspended". Preemptive wait types also weren't listed in SQL Server 2005, but the associated task status was marked as running. In SQL Server 2008, preemptive wait types are properly listed and their associated task status is also marked as running.

The names of preemptive wait stat types all begin with PREEMPTIVE_. Some examples you might see are PREEMPTIVE_ABR, PREEMPTIVE_OS_SQLCLROPS, and PREEMPTIVE_XE_DISPATCHER. There are a wide variety of preemptive wait types. If you see consistently high values in the preemptive wait types, I strongly suggest that you look into the wait type and try to find the root cause.

Multi-Tasking Potential Problems

When you go to school, you hope for a good teacher. When starting a new job, you hope for a good boss. Sometime one person with coordination authority can make life great or sometimes just the opposite. Similarly, in non-cooperative (preemptive) scheduling one entity decides when and where all tasks will receive resources. The scheduling must be balanced and smart to maintain a smooth running system. The risk is that preemptive can create some problems for execution of the tasks.

Preemption is act of an OS temporarily interrupting an executing task because it thinks a higher priority task is running. Here is a quick example of how tasks can get more or less attention. Suppose you have two windows open and both are loading multi-media. You minimize application A and bring application B to the foreground. The OS oftentimes boosts the priority of the active program (i.e., the one running in the foreground) over the background applications. Higher priority tasks can preempt lower priority tasks.

The OS usually lets SQL do its own thing and SQL uses cooperative multi-tasking. Sometime SQL wants to interact with OS level tasks, so the preemptive mode is used in SQL Server for external code calls. Most commonly the CLR with UNSAFE assemblies (see *SQL Interoperability Joes 2 Pros* Chapter 9 for more on UNSAFE CLR assemblies in SQL Server). APIs from extended stored procedures are another area where SQL tasks will need to be managed partially by the Preemptive scheduler of the OS. Those far-reaching tasks could be blocked for long periods of time.

Reducing Multi-Tasking Waits

Non-cooperative behavior can create multiple issues. The naming convention of the preemptive multi-task wait types is:

```
PREEMPTIVE_<category>_<function or class name>
```

Based on the name, we can find out which tasks are displaying non-co-operative behavior. The user should identify the task which is creating this wait type and optimize the query or procedure. There is no one answer which can fix this issue, as there are multiple reasons for this wait type.

Multi-Tasking - Points to Ponder

1. The SOS_SCHEDULER_YIELD occurs when a task voluntarily gives up execution for other tasks to execute. SQL Server has multiple threads to execute and does not let any "runnable" thread starve.

2. PREEMPTIVE Multi-tasking is non-cooperative. While SQL Server is executing a task, the operating system (OS) or other external process makes SQL Server yield. This kind of wait can drastically reduce performance and must be investigated.

3. Non-PREEMPTIVE multi-tasking is cooperative. When SQL Server manages the scheduling of threads instead of the OS, SQL Server decides the priority and one thread yields to another thread voluntarily based upon priority.

Chapter Four - Review Quiz

1) What is the purpose of the SOS_SCHEDULER_YIELD?

    O a. To make sure one thread completes before the next thread executes.

    O b. Voluntarily giving up execution for other tasks to execute and does not let any "runnable" thread starve.

    O c. It cooperates with external programs for CPU usage.

2) Which DMV should be executed to see the count of runnable task?

   O a. sys.dm_exec_sql_text

   O b. sys.dm_os_waiting_tasks

   O c. sys.dm_os_schedulers

3) What are the multi-tasking types in SQL? (choose two)

   □ a. Preemptive

   □ b. Multi-Threading

   □ c. Non-Preemptive

Answer Key

1.) SOS_SCHEDULER_YIELD voluntarily gives up execution for one task so other tasks can execute. This service is decided by SQL Server and not the operating system so (b) is correct. If one task ran to completion, all other task would have long wait times. Likewise if external programs have priority over SQL, then SQL waits, so (a) and (c) are incorrect

2.) The sys.dm_os_schedulers shows the active (runnable) task, so (c) is correct. sys.dm_exec_sql_text is run to translate SQL codes into text we can understand and sys.dm_os_waiting_tasks is to view the time a task waits to complete, so (a) and (b) are wrong

3.) PREEMPTIVE multi-tasking means the CPU is not shared. Non-PREEMPTIVE multi-tasking means that tasks take turns using CPU, so no one runnable task is starved for resources. Therefore, (a) and (c) are correct. Multi-Threading breaks up the workload to speed up a task, so (b) is incorrect.

Chapter 5. IO Waits

When you are not the one writing the check, it is very easy to suggest spending for better hardware. You often get pushback from people when you tell them their hardware is not as good as it can be. In reality, it is very difficult to convince an infrastructure team to change any hardware items because they are not performing at their best.

I had a nightmare related to this issue in a deal with an infrastructure team where I suggested that they replace their faulty hardware. This is because they initially would not accept the fact that their hardware was a problem. It is really easy to say "***Trust me, I am correct***", while it is more important that you articulate some logical reasoning along with this statement.

Most of the wait stats in the chapter are the kind that we can directly blame on the underlying hardware with a high degree of certainty. Nonetheless, it would be a good idea for you to take the extra steps to make sure of your conclusions. Keep in mind that when you ask a company to spend quite a bit of time and money on a live system, you really want to make sure you are correct.

PAGEIOLATCH_XX

Most of a table's space is occupied by records. Indexes and other properties use a relatively small amount of storage space. You may remember from the *SQL Architecture Basics Joes 2 Pros* book what a data page is in SQL Server. It's basically 8K of memory that stores data from a table. The more records in your table, the more data pages that table will need to use to hold those records. In short, as you add records to a table it takes up more memory pages. Data pages are the storage areas for data rows in tables.

Can two tasks access the same memory page at the same time? Yes, with some exceptions. It also depends what those tasks involve. Latches are small objects protecting transactions that need to be locked. While transferring a row to the SQL engine, the storage system must ensure that no other task modifies the data in the row. The storage system protects the row by acquiring a latch, loading the row in memory, and then releasing the latch.

The PAGEIOLATCH_XX is a suite of many wait stats about data page I/O completion. The reason for the XX in the name above is there are many different types of tasks that can hold a latch on a data page. We will cover more about this the types of tasks (update, insert, delete) later in this section and in great detail in Chapter 7.

Most PAGEIOLATCH_XX are the kind of wait stats that usually can be blamed on the underlying subsystem. Most of the time, that assumption is correct and the underlying subsystem is usually the problem. Simply put, this particular wait type occurs when any task is waiting for data from the disk to move to the buffer cache.

So what types of waits replace the xx in PAGEIOLATCH_XX? Starting with PAGEIOLATCH_EX, all of the definitions for the rest of this section occur when a task is waiting on a latch for a buffer in an I/O request and may indicate problems with the disk subsystem.

PAGEIOLATCH_EX

SQL Server requires a data page to be loaded into the buffer cache. SQL then allocates a buffer page to load and nothing else should be able to access it this during this time. SQL places the latch on the buffer page as the data is loaded from the disk. The latch request is in exclusive mode and needs an exclusive buffer page latch. Long waits may indicate problems with the disk subsystem.

PAGEIOLATCH_DT / PAGEIOLATCH_KP / PAGEIOLATCH_SH / PAGEIOLATCH_UP

The information and experiences recounted here represent what I have been able to assimilate so far on the challenging subject of latches. But there is a great deal more exploration and research needed before I can honestly say I understand these deeply.

KP stands for "Keep" latch and DT stands for "Destroy" latch. KP is compatible with all latch types except for DT. This means it is very "lightweight" and can be acquired with just about every latch type, except for DT. So what is a keep latch used for? Think of it as a "reference count" on the structure associated with the latch, such as a BUF. When a thread just wants to "look" at a BUF, it can acquire a KP latch and acquire whatever other latch type it needs (e.g., SH for "shared" (sometimes called "read")). The advantage here is that a KP latch ensures that no other thread destroys the BUF which it is trying to look at. This is because you need to acquire a DT latch in order to destroy a BUF. Notice that a DT latch is not compatible with any other type of latch. This makes sense because when you need to "destroy" the structure, you don't want any other thread to be able to access it.

So what does "destroy" means when talking about a BUF (i.e., a page)? One example is simply taking a BUF that is "clean" (not modified) and putting it on the free list of buffers to allow another thread to use it for a new page or a page to read in from the disk. Moving an existing BUF to the "free list" is a bit like getting rid of a page from a cache. We don't want any other thread even trying to access this page, so we issue a DT latch during this operation. If another thread then needed this page and it was removed from cache, the operation of reading it from disk would then kick in. Now you can see how a KP latch helps. It allows anyone to look at a BUF knowing it will not be destroyed "underneath it".

PAGEIOLATCH_EX Potential Problems

It usually does not take long to load data into a buffer. Oftentimes the loading of the data into the buffer comes from some task requesting the data. Once in the buffer, data runs very fast and many tasks can get this data quickly without any waiting. The only time tasks might have a wait is if 10 tasks request the same data at once. The first task might request the loading and the other nine must wait until the data is loaded into the buffer. If your disk is overwhelmed, then the first loading request might take too long. Also, if you have too little memory, your buffer might get purged too early and cause the next nine processes to re-load the same data upon another request.

Reducing PAGEIOLATCH_EX

While buffers are loading and unloading they will have a latch on the data. This means other processes must wait until the latch is released but the data remains in the buffer. Quick buffer loads and long lived buffers can help minimize waits. Just like any other wait type, this is again a very challenging and interesting subject to resolve. Here are a few things you can experiment with:

1. Improve your IO subsystem speed.

2. This type of wait stat can also happen due to memory pressure or any other memory issues. Putting aside the issue of a faulty IO subsystem, this wait type warrants proper analysis of the memory counters. If due to any

other reason, the memory is not optimal and unable to receive the IO data, thus creating a wait.

3. Proper placing of files is very important. We should check for the proper placement of files – LDF and MDF on separate drives, TempDB on a separate drive, hot spot tables on a separate filegroup (and on separate disk), and so forth.

4. Check the File Statistics and see if there is higher IO Read and IO Write Stall.

5. It is very possible that there are no proper indexes on the system (i.e., which causes a lot of table scans and heap scans). Proper created indexes can reduce the IO bandwidth considerably. If SQL Server can use an appropriate cover index instead of a clustered index, it can significantly reduce usage of CPU, Memory, and IO (considering cover index has much lesser columns than cluster table and all other it depends conditions).

6. Updating statistics can help the Query Optimizer to render an optimal plan. I have seen that updating statistics with full scan (again, if your database is huge, then don't attempt this) can provide optimal information to the Query optimizer and lead to an efficient plan.

7. Checking Memory Related Perfmon Counters
    o   SQLServer: Memory Manager\Memory Grants Pending (Consistent higher value than 0-2)
    o   SQLServer: Memory Manager\Memory Grants Outstanding (Consistently higher value, Benchmark)
    o   SQLServer: Buffer Manager\Buffer Hit Cache Ratio (Higher is better, greater than 90% for usually smooth running system)

- o SQLServer: Buffer Manager\Page Life Expectancy (Consistently low value)
- o Memory: Available Mbytes (Information only)
- o Memory: Page Faults/sec (Benchmark only)
8. Checking Disk Related Perfmon Counters
  - o Average Disk sec/Read (Consistent higher value than 4-8 millisecond is not good)
  - o Average Disk sec/Write (Consistent higher value than 4-8 millisecond is not good)
  - o Average Disk Read/Write Queue Length (Consistent higher value than benchmark is not good)

IO_COMPLETION

For any good system three things are vital: CPU, Memory, and IO (disk). Among these three, IO is the most crucial factor for SQL Server. Looking at real-world cases, I do not often see IT teams upgrading CPU and Memory. However, the disk is often upgraded for either improving the space, speed, or throughput.

In this section we will look at another IO-related wait type called IO_COMPLETION. The IO_COMPLETION wait occurs while a task is waiting for I/O operations to complete that are related to non-data page I/Os. With the IO_COMPLETION wait type you have an I/O bottleneck. You may see this wait type for the long-running I/O-bound operations. Any tasks are waiting for I/O to finish. This is a good indication that IO needs to be looked over to see how it compares to demand.

Reducing IO_COMPLETION

When you have an issue concerning the IO, you should look at the following items relating to IO subsystem:

Chapter 5. IO Waits

1. Proper placing of the files is very important. We should check the file system for proper placement of files – LDF and MDF on a separate drive, TempDB on another separate drive, hot spot tables on separate filegroup (and on separate disk), etc.

2. Check the File Statistics and see if there is higher IO Read and IO Write Stall.

3. Check the event log and error log for any errors or warnings relating to IO.

4. If you are using SAN (Storage Area Network), check the throughput of the SAN system as well as the configuration of the HBA (Host Bus Adapter) Queue Depth. In one of my recent projects, the SAN was performing really badly but the SAN administrator did not believe it. After some investigations, he agreed to change the HBA Queue Depth on the development (test environment) set up. As soon as we changed the HBA Queue Depth to a much higher value, there was a sudden big improvement in the performance.

5. It is very possible that there are no proper indexes in the system and there are lots of table scans and heap scans occurring. Creating proper indexes can reduce the IO bandwidth considerably. If SQL Server can use an appropriate covering index instead of a clustered index, it can effectively reduce lots of CPU, Memory, and IO (note that this advices assumes the covering index has fewer columns than the cluster table).

6. Checking Memory Related Perfmon Counters

   o SQLServer: Memory Manager\Memory Grants Pending (Consistent higher value than 0-2)

- o SQLServer: Memory Manager\Memory Grants Outstanding (Consistent higher value, Benchmark)
- o SQLServer: Buffer Manager\Buffer Hit Cache Ratio (Higher is better, greater than 90% for usually smooth running system)
- o SQLServer: Buffer Manager\Page Life Expectancy (Consistently low value)
- o Memory: Available Mbytes (Information only)
- o Memory: Page Faults\sec (Benchmark only)
- o Memory: Pages\sec (Benchmark only)

7. Checking Disk Related Perfmon Counters

- o Average Disk sec\Read (Values consistently higher than 4-8 millisecond are not good)
- o Average Disk sec\Write (Values consistently higher than 4-8 millisecond are not good)
- o Average Disk Read\Write Queue Length (Values consistently higher than benchmark are not good)

When a DML statement modifies records, the modified memory pages will be physically stored later, so that no excess time will be spent on the DML operation. The physical data modifications can happen a long time after the DML transaction finished, since that data is written to the log first. This means the write performance of your log data is very important.

The problem can happen when the time comes to write your log data to the pages on your datafile(s). These writes to your datafile(s) can affect the performance of your writes to the log for more incoming transactions. Also, when writing to the datafile(s) with new data (dirty records) from the log, this can slow down reads when selecting data on the same storage device.

If you are used to mowing your lawn weekly in the summer time, what happens when you come back from a two week vacation? It takes you longer to finish that task and you probably have to empty the grass catcher many more times. Your log activity may run into a similar situation if there are checkpoints which haven't happened for awhile. You will have more dirty records to load into storage at one time. You may notice times when your transaction per second takes a sudden drop even though drive activity might be increasing. The log may hit a checkpoint to dump all its dirty records to the disk with such a high priority that it must happen immediately. For that short moment, your physical activity focuses on one task and ignores new transactions.

This is why IO performance is vital. Naturally if IO is reduced, you would expect transactions to down. By monitoring IO performance and noticing the activity goes up while transaction per second goes down, you can identify this phenomenon. One way to reduce this is with an advanced storage system that can satisfy log I/O requests from cache. You can also split your read and write operations (if possible) to separate storage devices.

ASYNC_IO_COMPLETION

This wait relates to tasks which are waiting for I/O to finish. If the application that is connected to SQL Server is processing the data very slowly, this type of wait can occur. Several long-running database operations like BACKUP, CREATE DATABASE, ALTER DATABASE or other operations can also create this wait type.

ASYNC_IO_COMPLETION Potential Problems

When you encounter an issue related to IO, check the following items associated to the IO subsystem:

1. Look at the programming and see if there is any code which processes data slowly (e.g., inefficient looping). Code should be re-written to avoid this wait type.

2. Proper placing of files is very important. We should check the file system for proper placement of the files – LDF and MDF on separate drive, TempDB on another separate drive, hot spot tables in separate filegroups (and on separate disks), etc.

3. Check the File Statistics and see if there is a higher IO Read or IO Write Stall.

4. Check event log and error log for any errors or warnings related to IO.

5. If you are using a SAN (Storage Area Network), check the throughput of the SAN system, as well as configuration of the HBA Queue Depth.

6. It is very likely that there are no proper indexes on the system and thus there are lots of table scans and heap scans occurring. Creating indexes properly can reduce the IO bandwidth considerably. If SQL Server can use an appropriate covering index instead of a clustered index, it can effectively reduce lots of CPU, Memory, and IO (covering indexes generally have fewer columns than a clustered table).

Reducing ASYNC_ IO_COMPLETION

Here are a few counters to pay attention to when seeking to reduce this wait type:

1. Checking Memory Related Perfmon Counters

   o SQLServer: Memory Manager\Memory Grants Pending (Values consistently higher than 0-2)

   o SQLServer: Memory Manager\Memory Grants Outstanding (Consistently higher values, Benchmark)

   o SQLServer: Buffer Manager\Buffer Hit Cache Ratio (Higher is better, greater than 90% is preferred for a smooth running system)

   o SQLServer: Buffer Manager\Page Life Expectancy (Consistently low values)

   o Memory: Available Mbytes (Information only)

   o Memory: Page Faults/sec (Benchmark only)

   o Memory: Pages/sec (Benchmark only)

2. Checking Disk Related Perfmon Counters

   o Average Disk sec/Read (A value consistently higher than 4-8 milliseconds is not good)

   o Average Disk sec/Write (A value consistently higher than 4-8 milliseconds is not good)

   o Average Disk Read/Write Queue Length (Values consistently higher than benchmark are not good)

IO Waits - Points to Ponder

1. When suggesting upgrades due to IO Waits, we should be very sure of our suggestion before a company spends the large amount of time and money on these upgrades.

2. The PAGEIOLATCH_XX is a suite of many wait stats for data page I/O completion. This particular wait type occurs when a task is waiting for data to move from the disk to the buffer cache.

3. The IO_COMPLETION wait occurs while a task is waiting for I/O operations to complete that are related to non-data page I/Os. If your system has an IO_COMPLETION wait type, then you have an I/O bottleneck.

4. ASYNC_IO_COMPLETION waits occur if an application that is connected to SQL Server is processing the data very slowly. This happens when tasks are waiting for I/O to finish. To reduce these types of waits, check for: code inefficiencies; files split on separate disks; check I/O statistics, network throughput may be slow; and of course, you should check for proper indexing.

Chapter Five - Review Quiz

1) Data cannot be accessed by two or more tasks at once.

O a. True
O b. False

2) If there is a wait due to a latch on data, what kind of wait is it?

O a. IO_COMPLETION
O b. ASYNC_IO_COMPLETION
O c. PAGEIOLATCH_XX

3) Name the wait if an application connected to SQL Server is processing data slowly:

O a. PAGEIOLATCH_XX
O b. ASYNC_IO_COMPLETION
O c. IO_COMPLETION

4) Your system always seems to wait for disk writes. This type of wait is known as:

O a. PAGEIOLATCH_XX
O b. IO_COMPLETION
O c. ASYNC_IO_COMPLETION

Answer Key

1.) Data can be accessed by multiple tasks depending on the type of latch on the buffer, which makes (a) the correct answer.

2.) The correct wait for this would be PAGEIOLATCH_XX, since it is the only item dealing with latches.

3.) If you have verified that an application is connected to SQL Server but when the application tries to process the data it is slow, then you have an ASYNC_IO_COMPLETION wait. Answer (b) is correct.

4.) The type of wait described is an I/O bottleneck. IO_COMPLETION wait occurs while waiting for I/O operations related to non-data page I/Os to complete. Answer (b) is correct.

Chapter 6. Backup and Restore Waits

System backups are the single most important task performed by a database admin (DBA). Your data is at risk if you are not routinely performing database backups. Honestly, I have seen many DBAs who know how to take backups but do not know how to perform a system restore. (Sigh!)

Most of the time you don't really wait for backups. We don't expect them to be lightning fast, and they run on their own in the background. There are many different backup types and backup devices. Waits associated with a backup are rare, but you should be on the lookout for them. Backups are vital to all organizations that rely upon their data. You can offer tips on how to make backups better but you can never turn them off completely.

SQLAuthority.com
Joes2Pros.com

BACKUPIO and BACKUPBUFFER

These wait types occur when a backup task is waiting for the data or for the backup buffer. When I first encountered a client experiencing an issue with BACKUPIO, I initially had no idea how to resolve the issue. However, after troubleshooting the same issue for subsequent clients, I have a better sense of the problem environment. While I'm happy in my discovery, in reality the fix we used is not a true solution but a workaround (workarounds are never optimal but are sometimes necessary).

Reducing BACKUPIO and BACKUPBUFFER

These backup wait stats will occur when you are using a slow backup system. For example, tape backups can be extremely slow, particularly when a task must wait for a tape mount.

On a recent consultation, the backup to tape was very slow because the tape system was quite old. When I explained this wait type reason, the owners immediately decided to replace the tape drive with an alternate system. Fortunately they did not have to spend any money to try out the solution. They already had a small SAN (storage area network) on site which wasn't being used and which they decided to utilize for this test. One week later, I received an email from their DBA, saying that the wait stats had reduced drastically.

At another location, my client was using a third party tool (which I prefer not to mention by name) to take backups. One feature of this tool is that it compresses the backup while the backup process runs. I've always had good success with this tool except for this one outlying experience. When I took a backup using the native SQL Server compressed backup, the wait was low and the backup was much faster. However, when I attempted with the third party backup tool, the wait value again became very high and took much more time.

The third party tool had many other heavy features but this extra load was a waste to them, because the client was not using these features. We ended up using the native SQL Server compressed backup and it worked very well. If I am able to observe this situation more often in my future work, it will be an opportunity to understand this wait type in greater detail and formulate a more robust solution.

Backup and Restore Waits - Points to Ponder

1. Backup and restore waits can occur due to outdated backup devices, such as tape backup.

2. If a third party backup tool is used, check the settings to see if there are unneeded options selected, which can make the process take longer.

Chapter Six - Review Quiz

1) Should backups be taken offline?

  O a. No, the system should only be disabled to fix an issue, not for routine tasks, such as backups.
  O b. Yes, we only need backups when there is a problem.

2) Should backups ever cause a wait?

  O a. Yes, long enough to create the backup.
  O b. No, ideally they should run in the background.

3) If you discover a backup wait with a third party tool, what should you do?

- O a. Accept the wait, since the tool knows what it needs to create a backup.
- O b. Check the settings for the tool.
- O c. Check for other issues.

4) If there are backup waits and the client has its own backup system, what should be checked?

- O a. The network connection.
- O b. The speed at which the backup device runs.
- O c. The space available on the backup device.

Answer Key

1.) The correct answer is no (a). If a backup task is performed offline, it should only be long enough to fix or modify the task. If you wait until there is a problem to take a backup, then it is too late.

2.) Since backup tasks should be able to run without being noticed, the correct answer would be no (b).

3.) When a client uses a third party tool for backups, it is usually because the client was sold on all the "bells and whistles" the tool offers. These "bells and whistles" may be very useful, but remember that they can also hinder performance. The correct answer is (b).

4.) Many times people will upgrade the database (more memory, better IO, or even upgrade the CPU) but since the backup device has been working for them, they forget that it also should be upgraded. Although all the answers seem correct, you first need to check the speed of the backup device. The correct answer is (b).

Chapter 7. Locking Waits

We know multi-tasking is cooperative when SQL is sharing its resources. That is why two sessions (SPIDs) can simultaneously run queries against the same table just fine. Two queries on the dbo.Employee table at the same time work well. One query does not lock the other out. What would be unfortunate is if a third connection were to come in and drop the entire database. SQL won't allow that third connection to perform its drastic task until all other sharing tasks are done. This is because even something as simple as a query issues a shared lock on its underlying objects. One philosophy underlying SQL's sharing policy is that permissioned users can all come to the party as long as they don't take the punch bowl away. Locks are SQL Server's way of enforcing this rule.

Locking is a safeguard against bad things happening to the object you are using. In the case of shared locks, it does not prevent the usage of a table or row but keeps it safe from harm. Some operations will cause SQL to issue an exclusive lock, which means that nobody else can touch this data in any way until that exclusive locking task is done. Either way, you can say that locking is a mechanism used by the SQL Server Database Engine to synchronize access by multiple users to the same piece of data, at the same time. In simpler words, it maintains the integrity of data by protecting – or preventing – access to the database object.

LCK_M_XXX

If an UPDATE transaction on a record begins to execute, there are a few reasons why that update might not complete. If you enter a value that is too high, a trigger could roll back your changes. For example, the Yearly Salary field of the dbo.Payrates table will not accept a value of $1,000,000 because it exceeds the company limit. Suppose this update gets rejected by SQL because of an after trigger on the PayRates table. Although this value will never be accepted by the table (i.e., will never be persisted), before the rollback there is a fraction of a second when the value of $1,000,000 will be sitting in memory. For this reason, updates must disallow anyone else use of this data until the update succeeds or fails. Therefore, UPDATE statements need a more aggressive type of a lock than other types of DML statements.

SELECT statements require less locking. SELECT statements have no changes to make and therefore additional SELECT queries can run on the same table at the exact same time. When you delete a record, it means no one is going need that record. Since nobody needs the record, the DELETE statement uses an exclusive lock.

This chapter merely skims the surface of what locks are and what they do. A detailed study of the many types of SQL Server locks could fill an entire book. That said, SQL DBAs should be familiar with a few lock types. Most locks like to warn other locks they are coming. For example, SELECT statements can't run at the same time as an UPDATE statement. Therefore, the SELECT statement must wait until the update completes. But what if the update is also waiting and not using the table? The update is basically next in line. So you have a SELECT task waiting for an UPDATE task, which is also waiting. The UPDATE task has not yet generated an exclusive lock but it intends to. SQL issues an IX (intent exclusive) lock for the update, so it does not lose its place in line and other processes know they have to wait.

You can tell if a resource will be locked and by what type even before it happens. For example, every update lock starts off as an intent update exclusive lock. Once the intent process is over and the lock has been granted by the resource, the intent becomes the actual update exclusive lock.

I think the explanation of the LCK_M_XXX wait type is the simplest. When any task is waiting to acquire a lock on any resource, this particular wait type occurs. The common reason for the task to be waiting is that another task got there first. In order to lock a resource, it (the resource) must first have all other exclusive locks from other tasks released. This wait also indicates that resources are not available or are otherwise occupied at the moment. There is a good chance that waiting queries will start to time out if this wait type is very high. Client applications may also experience degraded performance.

The LCK_M_XXX wait types are summarized below:

LCK_M_BU - The task is waiting to get a Bulk Update (BU) lock.

LCK_M_IS - The task waiting to get an Intent Shared (IS) lock.

LCK_M_IU - The task is waiting to get an Intent Update (IU) lock.

LCK_M_IX - The task is waiting to get an Intent Exclusive (IX) lock.

LCK_M_S - The task is waiting to get a Shared lock.

LCK_M_SCH_M - The task is waiting to get a Schema Modify lock.

LCK_M_SCH_S - The task is waiting to get a Schema Share lock.

LCK_M_SIU - The task is waiting to get a Shared with IU lock.

LCK_M_SIX - The task is waiting to get a Shared with IX lock.

LCK_M_U - The task is waiting to get an Update lock.

LCK_M_UIX – The task is waiting to get an Update with IX lock.

LCK_M_X - The task is waiting to get an Exclusive lock.

LCK_M_XXX Potential Problems

One helpful way to think about the locks your database places on objects relates to the factors involved with road construction projects. A road can temporarily be merged into one lane to allow space for equipment and for the workers to operate. If they want the construction to get done twice as fast, then they block off two lanes. An entire road may even be temporarily shut down. We are more inconvenienced, but blocking more lanes means the overall project gets done faster. When the construction process finishes, then we will have a better road and be able to commute more efficiently than we did before.

So which option is better – the one where the construction crew blocks off the entire road and finishes faster, or where the road is partially blocked and it takes longer for the project to complete? "Better" can be a relative concept. If you need to get to the hospital quickly during construction, you prefer the partially open road so that you don't have to make a lengthy detour. On the other hand, your town collectively looks forward to having the road improved and would prefer that the construction team be granted exclusive use of the road in order to finish sooner. Closing the road so that the project can complete faster can also make the construction costs cheaper. However, if shutting down the road would cut off the town's main supply or commerce route for an unacceptable length of time, then the town's management has to look at the entire picture and decide what will be most beneficial for the town overall.

One cool feature about locks is that, to delete one record in a table of millions of records, you only need to lock the memory page of that one record. This allows multiple deletes to potentially run against the same table, as long as those records are in different memory pages (and they likely are).

Locking just one key in a table is cheaper than locking the whole table. However, when a large number of records need to be locked, this requires a different calculus. When you get enough records impacted by one task, eventually it's easier to involve the whole table and not just the individual rows. Consider that carrying a single cup (8 ounces) of water is easier than carrying a gallon jug (there are 16 cups to a gallon). It's even easier to carry two cups of water than a gallon jug. But carrying the gallon is easier than trying to carry three or more cups of water.

If you are deleting 500 records from a table containing 1,000,000 records, SQL has to make a decision. Are 500 key locks still easier than a single table lock? Since locking an entire table is cheaper than many small locks, SQL performs an escalation lock.

Reducing LCK_M_XXX

Lock escalation happens when many small page locks (granular locks) turns into a table lock. Even though you don't need the whole table, this lock has proven to be cheaper with respect to CPU time. Microsoft SQL Server performs lock escalation at times where it would improve overall performance. This may trigger lock escalation at a time when it is not desirable and may block other processes.

Oftentimes deletes are just clearing out old data you don't need any more. This deletes are for space planning and it's not as critical to have these run quickly. The priority is on new incoming data (not deleting old data). New queries or new inserts should not be blocked by table level locks from a delete operation.

Deleting the oldest 1,000 records might place an escalated lock on the whole table. Deleting 1,000 rows from a table might take two seconds with a table lock or 10 seconds with a thousand granular locks. If you allow the table to be completely locked, then live processes are blocked for two seconds. It might be better to have SQL spend 10 seconds deleting the old records in stages on data that nobody cares about. It will take longer to finish the deletes this way, but no live processes will be blocked.

It's a good idea that you read up on preventing lock escalation on MSDN before making any changes to your production server. As a last resort, you can take control of locking escalation with the following two DBCC TRACEON statements:

DBCC TRACEON (1211, -1) - Disables lock escalation and will not escalate row or page locks to table locks.

DBCC TRACEON (1224, -1) - Disables most lock escalation but the Database Engine escalates row or page locks to table locks if the amount of memory used exceeds certain conditions.

Locking Waits - Points to Ponder

1. Locking is a safeguard against bad things happening to the object you are using.

2. There are two main types of lock SQL Server uses. The first is a shared lock that allows multiple users to access the same data with no worry of the data being changed. The other type is exclusive where SQL Server performs an update or delete.

3. There are many types of Lock Waits associated with the locks SQL Server uses.

4. You can take control of locking escalation with the following two DBCC TRACEON statements.

    o   **DBCC TRACEON (1211, -1)** - Disables lock escalation and will not escalate row or page locks to table locks.

    o   **DBCC TRACEON (1224, -1)** - Disables most lock escalation but the Database Engine escalates row or page locks to table locks if the amount of memory used exceeds certain conditions.

Chapter Seven - Review Quiz

1) If two or more queries are accessing the same data, what type of lock is on the data?

   O a. Shared lock
   O b. Intent exclusive lock
   O c. Exclusive lock

2) While SQL is updating a record, you can still have access to this record.

   O a. True
   O b. False

3) Which Database Console Commands will allow you to control the locking waits?

   ☐ a. DBCC CHECKDB
   ☐ b. DBCC TRACEON (1224, -1)
   ☐ c. DBCC TRACESTATUS
   ☐ d. DBCC TRACEON (1211, -1)

Answer Key

1.) If more than one task is trying to access data then there is a shared lock, so (a) is correct. If a query is updating or deleting a record, then there is an exclusive lock until this task is complete.

2.) False. Anytime that SQL thinks that the data accessed may be dirty, SQL puts a lock on this data until it has been committed.

3.) Answers (b) and (d) are correct. But before executing these commands, you must research and understand how these commands affect your system. *This must be used as a last resort.*

Chapter 8. Database Log Waits

Most readers of this book probably already know what a log file is and what it is used for. Many SQL professionals know about these files but often just a fraction of their true usefulness.

In my experience, many students do not find the concept of log file activity an intuitive one. We will ease into it with some explanation that I've found helps people grasp this topic more quickly. But first we need a little explanation as to why SQL Server uses data files and log files.

Data Files and Log Files

SQL Server stores its data much like other applications – in files which are saved to a persistent drive. A distinguishing feature of SQL Server is its robust ability to keep track of things. *The security and safety of your data and reliability of your system are SQL Server's top priorities.* Therefore, you can imagine that logging activity – which tracks every transaction made in your database – is a pretty big deal. Examples where logging saves the day generally involve a database restore or recovery need. Once a database backs itself up, you're generally assured a reliable mechanism you can use to restore the system in case something unfavorable happens.

Suppose you notice bad data has come into your system through one of your periodic feeds. In fact, this data is so problematic that your team decides they must restore the database back to the point a week ago before the bad data began entering the system. *Your periodic database backup is built using information provided by the log file.* Log files keep track of your database transactions and help ensure data and system integrity, in case a system recovery is ever necessary.

SQL Server databases consist of files which are stored on a hard drive. Actually, I should qualify that – at least 80% of readers are probably like me and the "server" which their instance of SQL Server runs on is their local hard drive. (There may be a few developers who have a network set up and who are already running SQL Server on a separate machine or disk drive.) I have several machines, but I have one dedicated laptop I use for my Joes 2 Pros work.

Now we're ready to tackle data files and log files. A data file is fairly straightforward – it contains all your current data. Suppose you've been making changes to JProCo's Employee table. If you could peek into the data file, you would find data identical with the result of **SELECT * FROM Employee**. However, it wouldn't tell you that an hour ago, you deleted an employee record, or that today at 9:45 a.m. your manager added a new employee record to the table.

I sometimes compare the data file to getting information from my ATM. Usually I'm happy with the data my ATM shows me (i.e., my current balance), and it always provides my data rapidly. But if I need to look back and see deposit or withdrawal information, the ATM can't help me. To see the transaction detail which has led to my current account balance, I need to look elsewhere. Log files are just like the transaction history shown in my bank statements, where I can find a separate transaction entry for every purchase, deposit, or withdrawal made.

For student readers still trying to get their heads around this idea of data files and log files, have no fear – the video demonstrations from Chapter 1 of *Joes 2 Pros* Volume 3 contain many examples. These videos can be found here: www.joes2pros.com/videos/SQL-Architecture-Basics-J2P

WRITELOG Waits

WRITELOG is one of the most interesting wait types. So far we have seen a lot of different wait types, but this wait type is associated with the log file which makes it interesting to deal with. This wait type is usually seen in the heavy transactional database. When data is modified, it is written both on the log cache and the buffer cache. This wait type occurs when data in the log cache is flushing to commit the data to the disk creating a checkpoint, known as WRITELOG.

I recently saw this wait type's persistence at a client site, where one of the long-running transactions was stopped by the user, thus causing it to roll back.

Reducing WRITELOG Waits

There are several suggestions to reduce this wait type:

- Move the transaction log to a separate disk from the mdf (main data file) and other files.

- Avoid cursor-like coding methodology and frequent committing of statements.

- Check the IO-related counters (PhysicalDisk:Avg.Disk Queue Length, PhysicalDisk:Disk Read Bytes/sec and PhysicalDisk :Disk Write Bytes/sec) for additional details.

Logbuffer Waits

I initially didn't plan to write about this wait type. I've encountered it so infrequently that I'm not certain whether or not it is a common wait type. My research on this wait type continues, but I believe it probably is fairly rare.

A logbuffer wait occurs when a task is waiting to store a record in the log buffer. High values may mean the log device (your hard drive) cannot keep up with the amount of log activity.

Potential Logbuffer Problems

The log is usually has far less demands placed up on it than the load on the data files. A capacity failure would generally be found in a data file long before you would ever see this problem with a log file.

This assumption of the LOGBUFFER not being a problem before the load on the data files seems to be very accurate. On a system where I faced this wait type, the log file (LDF) was put on the very slow local disk, and the data files (MDF, NDF) were put on ultra-fast SanDrives. My client was then unfamiliar with recommended file distribution concepts. Once we moved the LDF to a faster drive, this wait type disappeared.

Reducing Logbuffer

There are several suggestions to reduce these wait stats:

- Move the transaction log to a separate disk from the mdf and other files. (Make sure the drive containing your LDF has no IO bottleneck issues).

- Avoid cursor-like coding methodology and frequent commit statements.

- You can also use sys.fn_virtualfilestats to find IO-related issues.

- Check the IO-related counters (PhysicalDisk:Avg.Disk Queue Length, PhysicalDisk:Disk Read Bytes/sec and PhysicalDisk :Disk Write Bytes/sec) for additional details. (You can read more about these at http://blog.sqlauthority.com/2008/02/13/sql-server-introduction-to-three-important-performance-counters).

- The following example displays statistical information for file ID 1 in the database with an ID of 1:
  SELECT * FROM fn_virtualfilestats(1, 1)

- The following example displays statistical information for all files in all databases in the instance of SQL Server:
  SELECT * FROM fn_virtualfilestats(NULL, NULL)

You may have noticed my suggestions for reducing the LOGBUFFER are very similar to reducing the WRITELOG wait type. Although the procedures on reducing them are alike, I am not suggesting that LOGBUFFER and WRITELOG are the same wait types. From the definition of the two, you will find their distinctions. However, they are both related to LOG and both of them can severely degrade the performance.

Database Log Waits - Points to Ponder

1. SQL Server is renowned for its robust ability to keep track of your system and data via logging activity. This is a reliable mechanism you can use to restore the system in case something a problem arises which impacts your data and/or your system.

2. The WRITELOG wait type occurs when data in the log cache is flushing to commit the data to the disk creating a checkpoint, known as WRITELOG.

3. Logbuffer waits occur if a task is waiting to store a record in the log buffer. In instances of high traffic or large transactions, the hard drive may not be able to keep up.

Chapter Eight - Review Quiz

1) What is the importance of the log file?

  O a. It records the activity on the server
  O b. Allows for a restore point in case corrupt data occurs
  O c. Both (a) and (b)

2) What is a WRITELOG wait created?

   O a. Anytime a record is updated

   O b. When the log cache is committing to disk

   O c. When SQL is recording an action

3) A Logbuffer wait happens when?

   O a. The memory is full

   O b. An application is accessing the server

   O c. When the disk is not fast enough for log data being pulled from the disk

Answer Key

1.) Log files give a detailed account of the actions executed on the server, including when they occurred. The log file can be used to restore the database should an unexpected error happen. Therefore (c) is correct.

2.) When a log record is flushed from the buffer and recorded on the disk but the disk is not fast enough, you will have a WRITELOG wait. Therefore (b) is correct. This is not only when a record has been updated. SQL first implements a log file in memory, so (a) and (c) are incorrect.

3.) Logbuffer waits pertain to the fact that the I/O speed is not fast enough. This makes (c) the correct answer. Logbuffer waits have nothing to do with whether an application is running or if there is not enough available memory.

Chapter 9. Waits on External Resources

A customer who uses SQL Server for all his operations had an interesting issue with a particular wait type. This customer had more than 100+ SQL Server instances running and we saw MSSQL_XP appearing as the most prevalent wait type occurring across the entire system.

I ran sp_who2 and other diagnostic queries, but I could not immediately figure out what the issue was – a query with that wait type was nowhere to be found! After a day of research, I was relieved to learn that the solution for this wait type is actually an easy one.

In this chapter, we will explore delays caused by external resources, such as MSSQL_XP (XP stands for extended stored procedure) and OLEDB Linked Server waits.

MSSQL_XP Waits

This wait type is created because of an extended stored procedure (XP). Extended stored procedures are executed within SQL Server; however, SQL Server has no control over them. Unless you know what the code for the extended stored procedure is doing, it is impossible to understand why this wait type is coming up. MSSQL_XP happens when a task needs to wait for an extended stored procedure to complete. The wait stops after the extended stored procedure call is done.

Reducing MSSQL_XP Waits

As mentioned above, it will be difficult to understand the behavior of an extended stored procedure, if its code is not available to you. In the scenario described at the beginning of this chapter, our client was using a third-party backup tool, which employed an extended stored procedure. Once we learned that this wait type being caused by the extended stored procedure of the backup tool, we contacted the third-party tech team (i.e., the vendor of the backup tool). The vendor admitted that the code was not optimal in some places, and within that day they provided a patch. Once the updated version was installed, this wait type disappeared. In other words, when we viewed the wait statistics of all 100+ SQL Server instances, the MSSQL_XP wait type had disappeared.

In simpler terms, you must first identify the extended stored procedure which is creating the wait type of MSSQL_XP and then try to get in touch with the creator of the stored procedure. Your explanation of the wait type occurring should help them optimize the code.

OLEDB Linked Server Waits

The OLEDB Linked Server wait is one of the top 10 wait types I have encountered in my performance tuning experience. This wait type primarily happens when a Linked Server or Remote Query has been executed. OLEDB (sometimes written as OLE DB or OLE-DB) stands for *Object Linking and Embedding Database.*

Reducing OLEDB Waits

The OLEDB wait type occurs when SQL Server calls the SQL Server Native Client OLEDB Provider. This wait type tends to become visible during the execution of a code on a linked server. SQL Server uses the OLEDB API when it retrieves data from a remote server.

When the remote system is not quick enough, or the connection between your SQL Server and the remote server is not fast enough, SQL Server must wait for the result to return from the remote (or external) server. This situation causes the OLEDB wait type to occur, and the wait tells you the duration of the calls made to the OLEDB provider.

These are the steps I use when I encounter an OLEDB wait type:

- Check the Linked Server configuration.

- Check Disk-Related Perfmon Counters:
    o Average Disk sec/Read (Values consistently higher than 4-8 milliseconds are not good)
    o Average Disk sec/Write (Values consistently higher than 4-8 milliseconds are not good)
    o Average Disk Read/Write Queue Length (Values consistently higher than benchmark are not good)

Waits on External Resources - Points to Ponder

1.   The MSSQL_XP wait type is created because of an extended stored procedure (an XP) executed in SQL and which SQL has no control over. Unless you can see and understand the code for the extended stored procedure, it is impossible to know precisely why this wait type is occurring. Reducing MSSQL_XP waits requires identifying the extended stored procedure and contacting its creator to request that the code be optimized.

2.   Object Linking and Embedding Database (OLEDB) Linked Server waits are caused by the remote system not being quick enough, or the connection SQL Server and the remote system not being fast enough. Check the Linked Server configuration or Disk-Related Perfmon Counters.

Chapter Nine - Review Quiz

1) What does XP stand for in the MSSQL_XP wait?

O a. The OS is Windows XP.
O b. SQL is waiting for extra power.
O c. Extended stored procedure.

2) What two things should be done to correct MSSQL_XP waits?

☐ a. Write a new stored procedure.
☐ b. Identify which extended procedure is causing the issue.
☐ c. Contact the creator of the stored procedure, so the code can be optimized.
☐ d. Disable the stored procedure.

3) What does OLEBD stand for?

O a. Objective link and embarked database
O b. Object linked and embedding data bridge
O c. Object linking and embedding database

4) What are the things you should check for with linked server waits?

O a. Average disk sec/read
O b. Network connection speed
O c. Linked Server configuration
O d. All of the above

Answer Key

1.) Similar to "SP" being the T-SQL keyword reserved for "stored procedure", XP is the keyword reserved for an extended stored procedure. Answer (c) is correct.

2.) Since extended stored procedures are in third party tools, and we have no access to them, the vendor of the tool needs to be contacted to modify the stored procedure code. So (a) and (d) are incorrect. The correct answers are (b) and (c).

3.) OLEBD stands for Object Linking and Embedding Database, so (c) is the correct answer.

4.) All the answers are correct, since this wait type can be casued by a bad connection between the two servers or by one system being slower than the other. Therefore (d) ("All of the above") is the correct response.

Chapter 10. DBCC SQLPERF

Taking the family to a new restaurant can be a fun adventure.
Think of a time you first visited a sit-down restaurant that had a
very large menu. While the idea of dozens (or even hundreds) of
possibilities is exciting, over repeated trips to this restaurant you
and your family most likely will end choosing from just a few of
favorites.

Diagnosing and troubleshooting a client's wait problems can be a
bit like that restaurant menu. Your first glimpse of all available
wait stats in SQL Server will be a little overwhelming, particularly
since they don't exist in a handy consolidated document with
concise descriptions (let alone prescriptions). A few quick internet
searches can be helpful, if you are really good at searching.
Similar to the restaurant visits, my experience over time has been
that most wait types are generated by a few "favorite" causes but
there will be "special occasions" where I need to explore a wait
type I haven't yet encountered.

As I mentioned previously, the new Denali version of SQL Server
adds a large number of documented wait types. There are also a
few types which have been discontinued.

DBCC SQLPERF(wait stats)

I received many comments, emails, and suggestions and for my recent blog series on wait types and wait statistics (which became the basis for this book). One frequent question was whether all of the discussions I have presented are also applicable to SQL Server 2000. I also received questions asking whether wait statistics matter in SQL Server 2000. If so, then the requestor wants to know how to measure wait types for SQL Server 2000. In SQL Server, you can run the following command to get a list of all the wait types:

```
DBCC SQLPERF(waitstats)
```

Because of backward compatibility, this query will also work in SQL Server 2005/2008/R2. As you may have noticed, I have been discussing everything with SQL Server 2005+ in mind and have given little specific consideration to SQL Server 2000. However, I believe that most of the suggestions I have provided are applicable to SQL Server 2000. While I would strongly urge any SQL Server user to upgrade and get the benefit of the newer version, the wait types I have been discussing mostly exist in SQL Server 2000, as well.

SQL Server Denali Wait Types

There are some restaurants we go to so frequently that don't need to see the menu. I was at one such restaurant where I knew my favorite meal and my favorite drink. That waiter said "I am sorry Sir, we no longer offer that drink, but we have some new ones you may like." My favorite drink was deprecated (discontinued) but new ones and a larger variety were there for the choosing.

A very common question I get is what new Wait Types will be included the next version of SQL Server. In other words what are the changes in SQL Server Denali with respect to Wait Types? Since I began discussing wait types and statistics on my blog, I have been receiving this question continually.

SQL Server Denali is yet to be finalized or released, so statements on this topic are preliminary and subject to change. I can tell you that the Denali CTP1 has been released, and I encourage all of you to download and experiment with it. I quickly compared the wait stats of SQL Server 2008 R2 and Denali (CTP1) and found changes where new wait stats were added and some old ones were deprecated.

Denali Deprecated Wait Types

Here is a list of wait types in SQL Server 2008 R2 that appear to no longer be present in SQL Server Denali:

QUERY_WAIT_ERRHDL_SERVICE
QUERY_ERRHDL_SERVICE_DONE
SOS_RESERVEDMEMBLOCKLIST
SOS_LOCALALLOCATORLIST
XE_PACKAGE_LOCK_BACKOFF

New Denali Wait Types

Here is a list of wait types in SQL Server 'Denali' but not in SQL Server 2008:

AM_INDBUILD_ALLOCATION
BROKER_DISPATCHER
BROKER_FORWARDER
BROKER_TRANSMISSION_OBJECT
BROKER_TRANSMISSION_TABLE
BROKER_TRANSMISSION_WORK
COUNTRECOVERYMGR

DBCC_SCALE_OUT_EXPR_CACHE
DISPATCHER_PRIORITY_QUEUE_SEMAPHORE
ENABLE_EMPTY_VERSIONING
FILESTREAM_CACHE
FILESTREAM_FCB
FILESTREAM_FILE_OBJECT
FILESTREAM_WORKITEM_QUEUE
FT_MASTER_MERGE_COORDINATOR
FT_PROPERTYLIST_CACHE
GHOSTCLEANUPSYNCMGR
HADR_AG_MUTEX
HADR_AR_UNLOAD_COMPLETED
HADR_CLUSAPI_CALL
HADR_DB_COMMAND
HADR_DB_OP_COMPLETION_SYNC
HADR_DB_OP_START_SYNC
HADR_DBSTATECHANGE_SYNC
HADR_FAILOVER_PARTNER
HADR_FILESTREAM_BLOCK_FLUSH
HADR_FILESTREAM_IOMGR
HADR_FILESTREAM_IOMGR_IOCOMPLETION
HADR_FILESTREAM_MANAGER
HADR_LOGCAPTURE_SYNC
HADR_LOGPROGRESS_SYNC
HADR_PARTNER_SYNC
HADR_SYNC_COMMIT
HADR_TRANSPORT_DBRLIST
HADR_TRANSPORT_SESSION
HADR_WORK_POOL
HADR_WORK_QUEUE
LOGPOOL_CACHESIZE
LOGPOOL_CONSUMER
LOGPOOL_CONSUMERSET
LOGPOOL_FREEPOOLS

SQLAuthority.com
Joes2Pros.com

LOGPOOL_MGRSET
LOGPOOL_REPLACEMENTSET
LOGPOOLREFCOUNTEDOBJECT_REFDONE
PREEMPTIVE_SP_SERVER_DIAGNOSTICS
PWAIT_ALL_COMPONENTS_INITIALIZED
PWAIT_HADR_ACTION_COMPLETED
PWAIT_HADR_CHANGE_NOTIFIER_TERMINATION_SYNC
PWAIT_HADR_FORCEFAILOVER_COMPLETED
PWAIT_HADR_OFFLINE_COMPLETED
PWAIT_HADR_ONLINE_COMPLETED
PWAIT_HADR_SERVER_READY_CONNECTIONS
PWAIT_HADR_WORKITEM_COMPLETED
PWAIT_MD_LOGIN_STATS
PWAIT_MD_RELATION_CACHE
PWAIT_MD_SERVER_CACHE
PWAIT_RESOURCE_SEMAPHORE_FT_PARALLEL_QUERY_SYNC
PWAIT_SECURITY_CACHE_INVALIDATION
QRY_PARALLEL_THREAD_MUTEX
QUERY_TASK_ENQUEUE_MUTEX
REDO_THREAD_PENDING_WORK
REDO_THREAD_SYNC
SECURITY_KEYRING_RWLOCK
SLEEP_MASTERMDREADY
SOS_MEMORY_TOPLEVELBLOCKALLOCATOR
SOS_PHYS_PAGE_CACHE
SP_SERVER_DIAGNOSTICS_INIT_MUTEX
SP_SERVER_DIAGNOSTICS_SLEEP
UCS_ENDPOINT_CHANGE
UCS_MANAGER
UCS_MEMORY_NOTIFICATION
UCS_SESSION_REGISTRATION
UCS_TRANSPORT
UCS_TRANSPORT_STREAM_CHANGE

XDES_HISTORY
XDES_SNAPSHOT
XDESTSVERMGR
XE_CALLBACK_LIST

We already know that Wait Types and Wait Stats are going to be the next big thing in the next version of SQL Server. I am eagerly waiting to dig deeper in the wait stats and look forward to keeping you all posted on my findings.

Chapter 11. Best References

Writing my blog article series on Extended Events was a great learning experience. Besides my blog series, there are excellent quality references available on internet which one can use to learn this subject further. Here is the list of resources (in no particular order):

- sys.dm_os_wait_stats (Books Online) – This is an excellent beginning point and official documentation on wait types in SQL Server.
http://technet.microsoft.com/en-us/library/ms179984.aspx

- SQL Server Best Practices Article by Tom Davidson – One of the BEST references available on this subject.
http://msdn.microsoft.com/en-us/library/cc966413.aspx

- Performance Tuning with Wait Statistics by Joe Sack – One of the best slide decks available on this subject. It includes many real world scenarios.
http://blogs.msdn.com/b/joesack/archive/2009/04/22/presentation-deck-for-performance-tuning-with-wait-statistics.aspx

- Wait statistics, or please tell me where it hurts by Paul Randal – Real-world notes from SQL Server Skills Master, Paul Randal.
www.sqlskills.com/BLOGS/PAUL/post/Wait-statistics-or-please-tell-me-where-it-hurts.aspx

- The SQL Server Wait Type Repository... by Bob Ward – A thorough article on wait types and their resolutions. Definitely a must read.
http://blogs.msdn.com/b/psssql/archive/2009/11/03/the-sql-server-wait-type-repository.aspx

Chapter 11. Best References

- <u>Great Resource on SQL Server Wait Types</u> by Glenn Berry – A perfect DMV to find top wait stats. http://sqlserverperformance.wordpress.com/2009/12/21/great-resource-on-sql-server-wait-types/

- <u>Tracking Session and Statement Level Waits</u> by Jonathan Kehayias – A unique article discussing wait stats and extended events. http://sqlblog.com/blogs/jonathan_kehayias/archive/2010/12/30/an-xevent-a-day-30-of-31-tracking-session-and-statement-level-waits.aspx

- <u>Wait Stats Introductory References</u> by Jimmy May – Excellent collection of the reference links. http://blogs.msdn.com/b/jimmymay/archive/2009/04/26/wait-stats-introductory-references.aspx

- <u>Performance Blog</u> by Idera – In depth article on the top wait statistics. http://sqldoctor.idera.com/tag/wait-stats/

Index

SQLAuthority.com
Joes2Pros.com

[THIS PAGE INTENTIONALLY LEFT BLANK]

Made in the USA
Lexington, KY
05 October 2011